AQUIRED BY GRAMMA
YARD SALE AND G
AFTER GRADUATION FROM

1986

Concepts of Criminal Law

Concepts of Criminal Law

Robert W. Ferguson
Saddleback College

and

Allan H. Stokke

Holbrook Press, Inc. Boston

Printed in the United States of America

Library of Congress Cataloging in Publication Data

Ferguson, Robert W 1940–
Concepts of criminal law.

Includes bibliographical references and index.
1. Criminal law—United States I. Stokke, Allan H., 1940– joint author. II. Title.
KF9219.F4 345′.73 76-000779
ISBN 0-205-04635-5

For our children,
Michelle and Bill Ferguson,
Eric and David Stokke.

Contents

Preface

Historically, members of the administration of justice system have been educated and trained in an atmosphere of almost total segregation from their subsystem colleagues. Law enforcement, judicial, legal, and correctional personnel have been educated individually with only a cursory coverage of the other members' subject matter. Criminal justice system personnel learned little of what the other members of the system were required to know; the result has been what sometimes appears to be a total lack of knowledge and understanding of the respective roles in the administration of justice. A common foundation of educational insights into the entire system greatly assists in developing understanding and sensitivity to the many difficult problems that face all members within the system.

The basic concepts of criminal law in this book can be compared to a basic criminal law book used in a typical law school, excluding the specific concepts and some detail that only apply to attorneys in their courtroom trade. The book contains legal history, methods of legal research, and basic concepts of law which, in past books, have received only cursory attention.

Because this book covers so many different concepts, it is by nature general. However, the information chosen for use in describing the topics is quite specific. Current research which best represents the knowledge amassed to date in the area of legal concepts has been selected and the research has been integrated into meaningful discussion.

It is our intent to establish a positive position upon a number of controversial issues. The material is designed for use in community colleges and state college-university criminal justice programs. The book is directed toward all members of the criminal justice system throughout the nation for the purpose of making the concepts of criminal law more familiar.

The book reflects the collective opinion of many professionals within the justice system. The authors recognize the impossible task of being all things to all people, and completely satisfying the numerous human opinions about every point within each legal concept. We have been sensitive to constructive evaluations from the field and have attempted to properly and fairly approach each issue.

The basic information supplied in this book will hopefully serve as a catalyst for continued research and greater understanding of the concepts of criminal law.

R.W.F.
A.H.S.

Chapter One

LEGAL RESEARCH AND METHODOLOGY

RAMIFICATIONS OF LEGAL RESEARCH

Legal research provides the answers to a multitude of questions facing criminal justice personnel, judges, attorneys, police, and correctional officers. Research into the law surrounding a particular problem gives the judge the tools with which he can render the proper decision. Research into the penal code and other sources provides an arresting officer an answer to the common question, "Now that I've arrested him, what do we charge him with?" Legal research helps the district attorney when he is faced with two different penal code sections which both seem to apply. Can a successful prosecution be carried out on the more serious of the two charges?

In the American system of justice, where both sides advocate their own positions as aggressively as possible, different interpretations to any given problem will frequently (and properly) arise. Both sides litigating as strongly as possible and both sides reinforced by appropriate case law and applicable statutes enable a judge to render a just and correct decision. A problem that appears to the police officer in the field to have a quick and easy answer may require a completely different answer later when the district attorney and defense attorney have carefully and thoroughly examined the law. Although conscientious criminal justice employees will strive to know as much as possible about the applicable law, they will still sometimes arrive at the wrong answer because fast action in the field is required in many circumstances. Legal research by a public officer, sometimes requiring no more than five minutes, can often provide the correct answer at the initial and most critical stage.

The important point is that legal research is essential and often determines the final outcome in a criminal case. One side failing to do the necessary research can cause them to lose the case. A police officer who does a brief amount of basic research at the beginning of a case may take action which later makes the difference between a guilty verdict and a not-guilty verdict.

During the developmental and fast-changing stages of search and seizure law in the 1960s, police officers who kept abreast of the law by reading summaries of new appeals from court cases were more successful than other officers; they knew what was allowed under the law as it currently stood. For example, in 1969, an officer reading *Chimel* v. *California*, 395 U.S. 752, would learn the limits of a proper search after arrest.

ORIENTATION TO CASE DECISION

"Case law," which is based upon case decisions, must be distinguished from "statutory law," which is based upon the acts passed by the state legislature and placed in the various codes.[1] It is these statutes, or code sections, that are often interpreted, modified, and changed by case law.

The molding and shaping of a set of facts and the blending of past cases with those facts in order to achieve a desired result is an art acquired by lawyers in law school and through experience. By examining the written opinion of a state supreme court, for example, one may determine what should be done in the present case in question, assuming there are some similar facts. (See Chapter 2 for an explanation of *stare decisis.*) An advocate attorney for one side will search for that case which is most similar factually to the case in question. Upon finding the best case, he should then check to see whether a later case has overruled it, or changed the ruling in any substantial way. The later case, if one exists, would generally determine the law, and the first case, though seemingly determinative, would be discarded; the law contained in it would no longer stand.

The law is dynamic and ever-changing; as our society and community changes, the law must also change to fit the new needs and problems that arise. The state legislature enacts, repeals, and amends statutes regularly as the needs of society demand; the courts of appeal and supreme courts likewise change the interpretation and application of those statutes as conditions change in the community. These changes in interpretation and application are reflected in case decisions coming from the appeals court.

Thus, one may see the historical development over a period of years of any particular subject under the law. For example, in 1900, evidence obtained in illegal searches, violative of the Fourth Amendment to the United States Constitution could still be used in both state and federal courts. However, society became more and more demanding than an effective means be developed to control police searches. The courts responded by interpreting the Constitution in such a way that by the 1960s, evidence obtained in unlawful searches simply could not be used in a criminal prosecution. The whole process of change took twenty or thirty years.

This dynamic concept of the law can be seen in areas other than constitutional issues. For example, at one time, if a death occurred during the course of the commission of a felony, the felon would be guilty of murder. Over the years, however, this theory changed so that now *only* felonies "inherently dangerous to human life" may be used as the basis for a murder conviction.[2]

For example, a chiropractor who commits the felony of grand theft by falsely stating that for $100 he can cure cancer is not committing an act inherently dangerous to life and would be guilty of manslaughter, not murder. The change came about because the courts concluded that it was simply not fair and just to hold a person guilty of murder in every situation where a felony has been committed and a death results.

As new cases are heard and argued, new opinions are written. It is this ever-changing aspect of case decisions that makes legal research important in the outcome of a case.

OUTLINE OF THE LEGAL BRIEF

At some points in legal history, written statements and arguments about the case were not required; an attorney would present his total case on appeal orally, taking whatever time he felt necessary. In modern times, however, all courts, including the United States Supreme Court, are too busy for this method to be practical. A written statement becomes essential, for it condenses the law and applicable facts into a package and does not require nearly so much time in presentation as would be required for a complete oral statement. The word "brief" means an "abstract" or "summary"; it should be complete but yet should not be exceedingly lengthy.

A brief serves several purposes:

1. To provide a complete documentation of applicable cases and statutes
2. To provide the public policy reasons and arguments favoring a particular result
3. To provide a busy appellate judge with a handy and simple book of reference; for example, a quick education on a particular point of law for someone who reads it

Proper legal briefs contain the following: a statement of the case, a statement of facts, the issues presented, the argument, and the conclusion.

The "statement of the case" is basically an introduction; it provides the reader with a history of what happened prior to the appeal and should also disclose the reason why the case is coming before the particular appellate court. The statement of the case spells out the parties and the procedural activity which took place. For example:

> In the Orange County Superior Court, before Judge D. Everett, the defendant,

> Jonathan Livingston, was convicted by jury on January 15, 1974, of grand theft and acquitted of receiving stolen property. Defendant was sentenced to State Prison when judgement was entered on February 2, 1974, and he now appeals from that judgement.

Only the essential dates and actions should be submitted.

The "statement of facts" serves the purpose of spelling out those facts which were admitted into evidence at the trial or other lower-court proceeding. Facts that were not introduced at the trial can *not* be mentioned unless they represented an exclusion of evidence and are claimed as an error on appeal. Generally, the statement of facts is a synopsis of the reporter's transcript; important facts should be spelled out in detail, possibly directly quoted. Minor, unimportant facts may be eliminated altogether. References should be made to the various points in the reporter's transcript so that one may easily find the original testimony on a particular point. Above all, the statement of facts should be accurate. Being clear and concise is also of utmost importance. Unfavorable evidence must also be mentioned even though it is detrimental. Opposing counsel would certainly direct the court to any omissions or errors. The statement of facts is not used for arguing the merits of the case. It would be improper to say: "The evidence on behalf of the defendant was strong in that. . ."

The "issues presented" section of a brief is short, but very important. Some attorneys feel that this section has more influence on the final result than the argument because the manner in which issue is framed can sometimes determine how the issue is decided. The following is an example of an appropriately defined issue: "Should the conviction be reversed where a defendant has been forced into trial over his objections and statements that he wants to have his attorney present?" The issue should not be stated in a general way, for that accomplishes nothing. For instance, it does not help at all to ask, "Was the evidence insufficient to sustain a conviction?"

The "argument" section of the brief allows one to write persuasively and imaginatively. The brief writer should not merely write down unsupported conclusions, he should bolster his argument with anything at all which lends weight: statutes, other appeals cases with similar facts, opinions of well-known and respected persons, and impressive quotations. Whatever is needed to influence and excite the reader toward the desired result may be used. The argument should be forceful and assertive. It should contain examples and references to specific facts. The writer should also use comparisons and analogies in order to create a favorable picture in the reader's mind. The argument should contain all of the most important cases from other appeals courts which have dealt with similar issues. Generally, one or two cases will be more significant than others. They should be analyzed in detail, and the appellate court should be shown how the case is similar and why it is just and proper to follow the ruling of the case.

If a case appears to be against the desired ruling, the attorney then carefully analyzes the case to discover the reasons why the case should be "distinguished," i.e., why that case is different from the case in question and thus, why it should be disregarded. Parenthetically, it should be noted that an attorney is ethically bound to bring to the court's attention all relevant cases—even those which could act against him. To do otherwise would be to mislead the court.

The writer of a good brief will develop every possible social and community policy consideration which supports his position. For example:

> In the interest of fostering and encouraging police officers to act quickly in emergency situations, the courts should not restrict an officer's forceful entry into a home when he hears violent screaming.

The writer attempts to lead the appellate court to the inescapable conclusion that if the ruling is not in the writer's favor, the community will suffer. The brief should relate the issue-at-hand to common, everyday circumstances so that the appellate court will recognize the impact on the community that a contrary ruling would have.

Such "public policy" considerations bear equal importance to the citation of case authority. Public policy can weigh heavily in both directions. For instance, in deciding the question of whether or not the state must appoint an attorney to represent a misdemeanor defendant, the desire to allow every accused person an attorney is weighed against the tremendous cost to the taxpayer that would be incurred. The interest in making sure every person has a fair trial with unbiased jurors is weighed against the practical problems of transferring cases to other counties whenever substantial publicity is involved.

So that there can be no doubt, the "conclusion" should state specifically what action is being asked of the appellate court, for example, "The judgment of conviction should be affirmed."

USE OF THE LAW LIBRARY

The user of a law library has one primary goal in mind: finding a pertinent law regarding the issue involved. In searching, a person must keep in mind the various tools of research contained in a law library. The basic tools and sources may be classified as follows:

1. The various *codes* containing legislative statutes
2. *Case reports* containing written opinions of cases decided by the Supreme Court and by other courts of appeal
3. *Digests and encyclopedias* classifying and discussing various issues of law and pointing out many of the cases which have discussed that issue in the past
4. *Law review articles* originating from the various law schools and discussing a particular issue of law in great detail
5. *Text books and treatises*
6. *Shepard's Citations*, containing the citation of all other cases that have mentioned the particular case or statute being considered

To understand the above reference tools, a person must know three things: 1. what is contained in the book, 2. how to "enter" the book to find the pertinent subject, and 3. how to move from one source book to another.

The codes contain statutes passed by the Congress or by the state legislature. Generally, a particular code section will show legislative history such as the original date of enactment, dates of amendments, etc. Most codes also provide cross references to other related code sections. Most important, however, are the annotations or brief notes which follow and refer to a particular code section. A good annotation section will contain a reference to every appellate case that in the past has had occasion to discuss the particular code section. A typical annotation to the burglary code section reads: "Mere possession of stolen property is not sufficient by itself to sustain a conviction of burglary, but such possession plus conflicting statements in explanation of that possession will suffice." *People* v. *Smith* (1956), 145 Cal App 2d 149, 302 P 2d 63. This example of an annotation was found under the "sufficiency of evidence" subsection in the annotations. The researcher has now "entered" one of the source materials and can now move into other materials in order to expand on this source and to follow it up to date.

First, the researcher reads the *Smith* case to be sure that it covers the subject he has in mind. If it comes close, he can then look for other cases cited in the *Smith* case and read those, or he can check the *Smith* citation in *Shepard's Citations* to find later cases which have cited and discussed the *Smith* case. The research person can also examine the head notes (summary) at the beginning of the case where he may find a reference to digest sections discussing this same issue. He has now moved chronologically backwards and forwards from the *Smith* case and has also consulted a digest which may lead him to additional cases.

The case reports contain complete written opinions of appeals in the United States Supreme Court all the way down to the lower appellate courts' hearing misdemeanor appeals. Frequently, several different companies publish the same opinion; the Supreme Court opinions are published in the official publication "United States Reports," in the "Lawyers' Edition," and in the "Supreme Court Reporter." These are abbreviated as "U.S.," "L. Ed.," and "S. Ct." Thus, a typical citation with reference to all three books is as follows: "*Chimel* v. *California*, 395 U.S. 752, 23L. Ed. 2d, 685, 89 S. Ct. 2034 (1969)." The number preceding the abbreviation is always the volume number and the number following is always the page number in that volume. The "2d" following the abbreviation merely indicates that this is the second series of volumes; the company merely went back to volume number one again and started over.[3]

Most publishers place "head notes" at the beginning of each opinion. Head notes are a one or two sentence synopsis of the court's statements on an issue decided in the case. These shortened versions, sometimes numbering three or four and sometimes numbering forty or fifty, should be used with extreme care, for they may be misleading or inaccurate due to their condensation. The head notes, however, can be used to see quickly whether or not the case covers the desired subject and to locate the pertinent areas in a long, involved opinion. As mentioned before, the head notes sometimes point toward a digest section discussing the same question.

It should also be noted that the majority opinion of the court will be preceded by the name of the judge who wrote the opinion. For example, "Smith, J." means that Justice Smith was the author of the opinion. At the end of the opinion will appear the names of the justices who concurred or dissented.

Dissenting opinions are occasionally written by a member of the minority of the court. Such opinions have only partial value as to their authority for a particular proposition. The opinions are important, however, in giving the researcher new ideas and new cases which may cover the desired subject. Also, it must be remembered that because of the constant changes which take place in legal theory, today's dissent may become tomorrow's majority.

The content of appellate court opinions varies, but basically each contains a description of the relevant facts followed by a review of relevant cases along with the application of those cases to the facts. Many opinions will also consider the public-policy reasons or consequences of the decision; for instance, if we do not allow a police officer to take this course of action, will he be able to enforce the law and do his job properly? Often a court will be required to balance the rights of individual citizens against the desire of the community to have laws fairly and effectively enforced.

The various digests are basically a means for indexing the various cases that discuss a particular point of law. For example, state digests will have a section devoted to criminal law, breaking that subject down into many subsections:

Criminal Law

II. Homicide

B. Defenses
  1. Self defense
    d) Defense of others

Thus, under the "Defense of others" heading would be grouped the various cases dealing with that subject. Some digests provide a synopsis of how the opinion reads on this subject, others only provide the name of the case and its citation. The function of the digest is to locate cases dealing with the subject, allowing the researcher to move from the digest to the case reports.

The digest is best approached by using the topical index or by already knowing the name of one case dealing with the issue in question. The topical index describes the various locations within the digest where cases will be grouped together involving the subject in question. Some digests use a descriptive-word index as well; for instance, a person may look at "dying declarations" in the index to find which digest volumes cover that subject. "Dying declarations" would probably be discussed in the "Evidence" section as well as in the "Criminal Law, Homicide" section. One may also use a digest by knowing the name of one case, finding it in the index of cases, noting the locations in the digest where that case is mentioned, and then looking at that other part of the digest. By so doing, one should find other cases on the same subject.

The digests are of four basic types:

1. All-inclusive digest covering all federal and state cases as far back as the 1700s and 1800s[4]

2. Regional digests covering the cases from several states in a particular geographical area[5]
3. Digests covering one court system, such as the United States Supreme Court[6]
4. Digests covering just one state[7]

There are many, many digests from which to choose; depending on the scope of the job to be done, the time available, and the difficulty of the problem, the researcher must decide which digest to use.

Encyclopedias describe and discuss the various propositions and principles of law. These essays on the various rules of law are topically arranged and also supported by footnotes containing case citations. The encyclopedia has a dual function: it can be used as a means for searching out additional cases dealing with the subject in question, and it can also be cited as the authority for a particular proposition.

Several types of encyclopedias are published:

1. Those which deal with nationwide case law from the first reported case to the present[8]
2. Those which cover only one state[9]

Generally, encyclopedias are entered by a topical index or through the table of cases cited in much the same way as the digests are used. Although the essays found may be cited as the authority for a rule of law, a person doing careful research will not depend solely upon what he finds in the encyclopedia; the case cited in the encyclopedia in support of the rule of law should be read and checked out to determine whether or not it has been overruled by a later decision.

Law reviews, often cited as authorities by persons doing legal research, are periodicals originating out of the various law schools, generally edited by the students and written by the students, faculty, and other contributing attorneys. Often a person with highly specialized knowledge obtained through study or experience will write in great detail about a narrowly defined subject of current interest. The article may contain the opinions and criticisms of the author along with citations to cases. These articles, often relied upon and referred to by courts and by lawyers, are found by using the *Index to Legal Periodicals* or some similar index and checking under the desired topic.

Textbooks and treatises sometimes prove helpful in finding additional cases. Also, if the researcher feels he has absolutely no knowledge on the subject in question, a textbook may provide him with the essential informational background that he needs in order to do the research. A treatise, needless to say, will not be generalized, as are many textbooks, and it will go into much more detail and contain many more cases discussing a particular field of law.

Shepard's Citations remain unique in the field of legal research. No other publication contains a quick and easy reference to all later cases which have mentioned the case a researcher has in mind. *Shepard's* is essential to a proper and complete job of legal research. Without using it, an attorney takes the risk of using a case which has been overruled by a later court decision, a cardinal sin for a lawyer to commit.

"Shepardizing the case," a phrase used by many lawyers, is done as follows:

1. The research person has before him the case of *People* v. *MacMullen* (1933) 134 CA 81. He has determined that the case is of help to him in his argument because the holding is that a husband and wife alone can not be convicted of conspiracy.
2. The person doing research wants to determine whether *MacMullen* is still good law. He finds "Shepard's California Citations, Appellate Court Reports, Case Edition, Part 2, 1970" which will cover the years from the date of the *MacMullen* case (1933) up to the date of this *Shepard's* book (1970).
3. Since "134 C.A." means *MacMullen* is located in Volume 134 of the California Appellate Reports, he turns to the section which has "California Appellate Reports" at the top of the page and "Vol. 134" at the top right. Looking down the page, he finds "Vol. 134" in large, bold print with the page numbers in Volume 134 also listed in bold print underneath. Reading down the column, the researcher finds page 81 with the following citations under it: "q 61 C^2d 882." The "q" means that in the case to be found at 61 C^2d 882, the Supreme Court of California questioned the *MacMullen* case. In reading the new case, the researcher finds that the supreme court questioned the *MacMullen* case to such an extent that it is no longer considered good law. The ruling now is that a husband and

wife *can* be convicted of conspiracy. The rule has changed.

4. Since other cases are noted under page 81, the researcher may also wish to look at them to see whether or not they add anything to what he has already found.

Many other points of information can be gleaned from a Shepardizing process. Under the page number of the case in question, one will find citations to all cases that have ever mentioned or discussed the case in question. A small "c" before the citation means that the case was criticized, and a small "o" means that it was overruled. A small "j" means that it was used in a dissenting opinion, while a small "d" means that the case has been distinguished.

The column of citations will also contain the citation of any law review article that discussed this case, as well as a reference to ALR (American Law Reports) articles. One can also find parallel citations, for instance, the *MacMullen* case is also reported in "24 P2d 794" (24th Volume of the 2nd series of Pacific Reporter System on page 794).

Shepard's citation system consists of one set of books for the various courts in each state and one set of books for such regional reporters as the Pacific Reporter. *Shepard's* also maintains one set of citation books for the United States Supreme Court wherein a person can take any one of the three reporter citations (U. S., S. Ct., or L. Ed.) and "Shepardize" it. The "preface," "analysis," and "abbreviations" found at the beginning of each *Shepard's* book is "must reading," for with study, the reader can see exactly how to use the book and with practice, it can be done quickly and efficiently. The preface must often be referred to in order to determine what the abbreviations mean.

Shepard's also maintains a set of books containing all case citations of a particular statute, code section, or section of the Constitution. "Shepard's (state) Citations, Constitutions, Codes, Statutes, Ordinances, Charters, Court Rules, Statute Edition, 1970," for example, can show a person the citation of every case that has mentioned the penal code section for burglary. Hundreds of cases are listed under that section.

Monthly supplements are published and, when large enough, are placed in one of the large bound volumes. A person using *Shepard's* must remember to check the most recent supplement as well as the regular bound volume.

This chapter, describing the use of a law library, contains the basic tools used in legal research. A person doing research will develop his own favorite methods as he gains experience. A favorite method of one person, may be unsuitable to another. However, both should come up with similar results, at least to the extent of discovering the same leading and most relevant cases and statutes dealing with the particular issue in question. Even though using different methods, two people should be able to find the same law.

Endnotes

1. Originally, criminal law consisted of various rules coming from England called the "common

law." Many of the "common law" crimes were adopted by the state legislature with certain modifications and now appear in the Penal Codes of various states. (For example, California Penal Code § 484 (theft) and § 187 (murder).

2. People v. Phillips, (1966) 64 Cal 2d 574, 51 C.R. 225, 414 P. 2d 353.
3. Thousands of abbreviations exist for books containing reported cases and legal articles. The following, for purposes of illustration, are some of the most common:

   A. Atlantic Reporter

   A.2d. Atlantic Reporter, Second Series

   A.B.A.J. American Bar Association Journal Abb.N.Cas.

   Abbott's Practice (N.Y.)

   A.C. Advance California Reports, A'Beck. Res. Judgm.

   A'Beckett's Reserved Judgments (Victoria)

   A.C.A. Advance California Appellate Reports, Abs.

   Abstracts, Treasury Decisions.
4. American Digest System.
5. Pacific Digest.
6. U.S. Supreme Court Reports Digest (Lawyers Co-op. Publishing Co.); U.S. Supreme Court Digest (West Publishing Co.)
7. West's California Digest; Callaghan's Illinois Digest.
8. Corpus Juris Secundum (American Law Book Co.)
9. California Jurisprudence 2d.

QUESTIONS

1. Why is legal research necessary in the administration of justice?
2. What is the difference between case law and statutory law?
3. Name several purposes of the legal brief.
4. Discuss the outline of the legal brief.
5. Name five resources found in the law library and discuss the value of each.
6. Interpret the case citation "*Chimel v. California*, 395 U.S., 752.
7. Explain what is meant by "Shepardizing the case."

Chapter Two

PHILOSOPHICAL AND HISTORICAL DEVELOPMENT

GENERAL AND SPECIFIC SOURCES OF LAW

The history of the law bears a direct relationship to the history of recorded civilization. Long before the birth of Christ, men formulated certain rules and procedures for resolving disputes and regulating conduct. The first laws were merely unwritten rules developed by the heads of individual families for the protection and function of that family. From that humble beginning, intricate legal philosophies grew.

Defining the philosophy and thoughts behind the formulation of law has always been a subject of controversy and sometimes of confusion. To truly understand the law, one must have some idea of why and how the basic principles of law developed. The objectives of the lawmakers or lawgivers must also be examined. In understanding the philosophy and history of law, it becomes apparent that the thinking of the past often influences the law, procedures, and institutions of the present.

Roscoe Pound describes two needs that can be seen as the controlling forces behind most philosophical thinking in the area of law. First is the social interest in maintaining security in the community and regulating and controlling governmental as well as individual activity. Second is the need to provide for and allow changes in law in response to expected or unexpected changes in the community, in other words, fitting the law to a situation which no one anticipated.[1] Clearly the two needs sometimes conflict; law should be stable and predictable, yet change must be allowed because all societies are constantly changing.

Several civilizations developed law which did not survive to any great extent into modern civilizations. In ancient Babylon, the code of Hammurabi was developed by King Hammurabi more than two thousand years before Christ. It was basically an "eye for an eye" code; if a victim suffered a physical loss, provisions existed for some kind of reimbursement by the state. Persons caught in the act of adultery were bound in that position and thrown into the river. In essence, the code was thought of as being a divine origin, certain rules for human conduct that were required by the gods.

The Egyptian civilization, of course, became highly developed; the professions of law, medicine, and religion were lumped together and administered by the priests. A few ideas were borrowed from Hammurabi, but most law was of Egyptian origin. The penal provisions were rather mild, and though a death penalty existed, it was often commuted to penal servitude or slavery.

Hebrew law, a large part of which was developed by Moses, borrowed in part from the code of Hammurabi as well as from Egyptian law. (It will be recalled that Moses was raised under Egyptian law.)

Hebrew also also provides a good example of the legal theory that law is of divine origin (the Ten Commandments, for instance). In Hebrew law, the "eye for an eye" theory was important, but fines were also used as punishment. Often, a criminal was required either to pay money to the victim or be sold into slavery. Most sexual violations were punishable by death, thus forming the historical basis for Hebrew-Christian strictness toward sexual activity. Though Hebrew law has had some effect upon modern thinking, Greek philosophy has had a much larger and far-reaching influence.

The history of law in ancient Greece in the fourth and fifth centuries B.C. again shows one of the first sources of law to have been of divine inspiration. The gods helped the king to decide a particular dispute. Later, the people saw what the king's customary decision was and eventually required that these traditional decisions be published in some form, thus establishing a body of law for all to use. Because of the participation in government by many of the Greek citizens, the laws of the time were constantly changing and individualized.[2]

One of the early Greek lawmakers, Draco, felt that the fact of a violation of law where a citizen violated the requirements of society, was of more consequence than the act itself. The commission of a crime constituted a blow against the government as well as against the victims. The Draconian code therefore provided that the punishment for theft was the same as that for murder. (The term "Draconian" in popular usage describes any law which is overly strict.)

Later, the legislator Solon revised the Draconian code into such a reasonable, well-working code that it lasted far beyond the fall of Greece. The code of Solon was engraved on brass tablets and placed in the market place for all to see so that all would know the law. The Greeks also formed a court, the Great Court of the Areopagus, consisting of nine to fifty judges, depending on the case. So good and respected were the decisions of this court that foreign states sometimes sent cases for arbitration.

Greek philosophy, as developed by Aristotle and others, helped to produce one of the major conflicts affecting the administration of justice. The distinction between law and rules of law has been debated over the centuries. Is the required conduct fair and just by nature, or is it merely required by convention or enactment? Aristotle defined the law as that which is fair and just by nature. The opposing theory concerns those enactments which are fair and just only because they come from convention or enactment.[3] In modern times, discussions of criminal law often use the terms *malum in se* (bad in and of itself) and *malum prohibita* (bad because it is prohibited) in describing these same thoughts. A modern example, would be murder (*malum in se*) as opposed to possession of marijuana and contracting without a license (*malum prohibita*). Some modern justice thinkers carry this philosophy to the point where they believe most *malum prohibita* crimes should not be enforced so that law enforcement personnel can devote more time to the "real" crimes, or those that are *malum in se.* The point at which this conflict will be resolved depends upon the courts, the legislature, and the demands of society. Greek philosophy in general advocated maintaining the general security through the security of social institutions. Law was a device which worked to keep every man locked into his particular part of society, thus preventing friction between that person and those from other segments of society.[4]

While in the beginning a civilization's law was a device and means for keeping the peace, the Greeks saw the law as a means of maintaining the social status quo. Plato and Aristotle fully developed this idea: a man was to be reclassified and assigned to a class to which he was suitable, and the law was then supposed to keep him there. The shoemaker should be a shoemaker and not also a judge; the soldier should not also be a businessman. When St. Paul told wives to obey their husbands and servants to obey their masters, he was not only asking each person to do his best in the class and position where society had placed him, but he was also setting forth the Greek idea of law.[5]

Following Greek civilization, the Roman Empire became the dominant force in the development of law. As may be seen, Roman theory and philosophy were still major forces even in the eighteenth century. Near the beginning of the Roman Empire, Cicero spelled out three elements of the law: legislation, administrative edicts, and judicial reasoning on the basis of legal tradition.[6] It was the latter source of law, the writings of judicial reasoning, that became the growing and most important area. These writings of legal tradition eventually became the Digest of Justinian, which for centuries was one of the sources of law to Romans and non-Romans alike. The basis of these traditional writings was reason and a sense of justice, possibly natural law.[7]

In these original legal writings can be seen the first examples of law preserving stability, yet allowing for change in response to the demands of society. The juristic writers were practical and reasonable; using the principle of natural law behind legal rule (ratio legis), they interpreted and molded the legislation and administrative edicts of the time in response to the current needs.[8]

The needs of the times had changed drastically as the world expanded from the city-oriented governments of Greek and early Roman civilization to the ultimately massive size of the Roman Empire. Writers were required to begin with basic rules of city government and to make them into an instrument for satisfying the needs of a whole empire, while at the same time maintaining uniformity and predictability.[9]

Roman legal philosophy also became a process for maintaining the status quo; by this theory one begins with certain opinions about what is best and what is good in a particular segment of society. What is considered best ends up in a body of law because society wants to maintain that status. That law is then used to measure and control all future situations or cases. The law over the years must be shaped and molded in order to maintain and further the ideal of the social status quo and to fit it to new situations.[10]

The Justinian code, formulated by Emperor Justinian in about 529 AD, contains many provisions later found in many other countries, including the United States. The code allowed for individual rights and property ownership, but yet the harmony of society and the social order could not be disturbed by an individual attempting to "do his own thing" if those actions conflicted with society. By Justinian law, all citizens must respect other individuals, what they own, and who they are. Another person must be allowed to use his property and other acquisitions without interference so long as he uses them within the defined limits.[11]

When the Dark Ages followed the breakup of the Roman Empire, no developments of any consequence occurred in the philosophy of law. Anarchy and confusion existed for hundreds of years. Education, philosophy, science, religion, and civilization itself were in states of hibernation.

In the Middle Ages, society demanded law, particularly a system of law which would counteract the anarchy and violence of the Dark Ages. Thus, strict authoritative law developed. Roman law was often used as a basis for the strict law that developed during the fourteenth and fifteenth centuries. The Roman law of Justinian was especially used. The social order, however, was now different, and changes and molding of the legal theory of the Romans occurred in order to fit it to the demands of this new society. The Roman idea of finding that which is good and maintaining it gathered new strength and flourished.[12]

Consider the importance of law in the fourteenth through the sixteenth centuries when commerce and trade were expanding and new worlds were being discovered. Natural law and the rule of reason again became the guiding principles in the development of law. Natural law, of course, claimed as its basis the premise that man is a rational creature.[13] During this period, individual thought and actions were encouraged; man no longer was required to stay in a given place in society.

Natural law, combined with a background of Roman law for stability, developed into English common law. The teachings and principles set forth in the Magna Charta, which spelled out the rights of individuals, had a great deal to do with English legal development. From the twelfth through the seventeenth centuries, the English developed certain devices and procedures to protect the rights of the individual. The jury trial came into being, although in early centuries, jurors were sometimes fined for making the wrong decision or even refused food until a decision was rendered. Professional lawyers also made their appearance at this time.

The writ of Habeas Corpus, the Great Writ, was drawn up and allowed any person held by the state to require that his captors show good cause why he was being held in custody. The writ has survived in English law (and later in American law) right up to the present; it operates by allowing a man in custody to file with a court a paper stating that he is being held in violation of the law or without just reason. The act of filing the paper then transfers the burden of showing lawful custody and lawful state acts to the state officials involved. If they cannot show lawful acts and lawful custody, the court must then order the person to be released. Without the writ, the state could hold a person in custody for years when there is only a hunch or groundless suspicion that the person ever committed a crime.

DEVELOPMENT OF COMMON LAW AND MODERN LEGAL PHILOSOPHY

In the eighteenth and nineteenth centuries, codification and classification of the law took place. Many of the codes on the continent were based on the French Code of 1804. Such codes marked a process of maturation in the development of law,[14] for industry and commerce had become more and more developed, countries required more stability and predictability, and business communities had to be able to demonstrate the validity of their contracts and their actions.

It was also in this context and period of time that our more important criminal legal theories were developed. Sometimes termed the fundamental maxim of the whole of criminal law,[15] the requirements of *mens rea* originally came from Roman law. *Mens rea* is the concept in criminal law which *requires a particular mental state before the concurrent act may be called a criminal act.* Since there can be a conflict between law and morals, it would be incorrect to state that legal guilt cannot exist without moral guilt being shown.

Great difficulty arises in analyzing *mens rea.* Can one say that the absence of *mens rea* on a particular occasion deprives what would otherwise be a crime of its criminal character? No. Two examples are pointed out: if a railroad man falls asleep and an accident results in the death of others, he may be guilty of manslaughter; if he deliberately uses a weapon to cause the same result, he is guilty of murder. Considering these examples, *mens rea* seems to be two states of mind, completely opposed to each other. One involves a passive state of mind, and the other represents an active desire to kill. Thus, it must be concluded that the true definition of *mens rea* means that the mental state varies depending on the definition of the particular crime. Thus, in theft, the *mens rea* is the intent to permanently deprive the owner of his property, while in murder it is a state of mind constituting "malice aforethought."[16]

Other concepts basic to modern criminal law came into maturity during the nineteenth century in

England. For example, in order to be held responsible for crime, (liable for punishment) one must have the knowledge that the act is wrong and the power to abstain from doing it. This concept forms the basic premise for most of the American and English theories of insanity defense.[17]

In criminal matters, wrote Jeremy Bentham in 1825, the accused is entitled to the presumption of innocence. Bentham concluded that in every criminal proceeding there is always a wrong committed by either the accused or by the accuser. In idle conversation, false accusations may arise, or because of religious persuasion or reasons of passion, a person may be falsely accused. Thus, it is better to let a guilty man escape than to take a chance on condemning an innocent one. Bentham notes that the danger arising from the acquittal of a guilty person will be greater than the dangers of convicting an innocent one; i.e. more thefts will likely occur. However, he maintains that this danger must be accepted as unjust punishment is the higher evil and must be avoided at all costs.[18] The presumption of innocence, along with the state's burden of proving the accused guilty beyond a reasonable doubt, have been jealously guarded in the last century or so, and both still exist virtually unchanged today. (Proof of guilt beyond a reasonable doubt overcomes the presumption of innocence and will result in conviction of the accused. "Reasonable doubt" must be distinguished from the proof needed in civil cases, which is a preponderance of evidence, a probability. Thus, to convict a person of manslaughter based on drunken driving, there must be proof beyond a reasonable doubt; the same person may be sued for damages in a civil court, and at that time, the plaintiff would need only 51 percent of the evidence [preponderance] in order to find the defendant liable to pay money damages. Money is not so important as a person's liberty.)

The common law as it is now known had its origins at the beginning of English history. In the twelfth century, Henry II, who inaugurated trial by jury (rather than trial by ordeal or duel) also set up a system of courts to administer law common to the whole land and to all men. As these primitive courts decided cases, a few judges kept notebooks of cases and writs. As new cases came along to be decided, it became only natural to look back to the older cases for assistance in making the decision. William Blackstone, in his *Commentaries on the Law of England,* written around 1765, distinguished the *unwritten,* or common law from the statutory, or written, law.[19] The common law of that time included general customs prevalent throughout the country as well as legal decisions. The law, described by Blackstone as being the common law of England, covered well over a thousand printed pages. He wrote that although the laws were not acts of Parliament, they still had binding power and the force of law simply because of their long and immemorial usage and their universal acceptance throughout the kingdom.[20]

The rules of law may have originated from Roman or Greek law, from the Danes or the Saxons, or from many other sources. Blackstone, however, felt that many of the maxims and customs that he collected were older than memory or history could clearly distinguish. It was this characteristic that made it the "common law." The "goodness" of a custom depends upon it having been used longer than man can remember.[21]

Blackstone described thousands of customs that

made up the common law. He described the relationships between master and servant, husband and wife, and parent and child. He also described the law surrounding the manner and form of acquiring and transferring property. He declared that a deed to land was of no validity unless it was sealed. All of these doctrines were never set down in any written statute or ordinance but depended upon immemorial usage—they comprised the common law.[22]

Blackstone also related how these customs or maxims were to be known and determined. The judges in the various courts of law were the depository of the law—the living oracles, he declared, who were bound by oath to decide a case according to the law of the land. A judge's knowledge of the law was attained by study, experience, and familiarity with the decisions of prior judges. Thus, the judgment and all court records in the prior cases must be maintained because reference must be made to those cases in order to decide the outcome of the present case.[23] Thus, it is the common law that is the father of the concept of *stare decisis* (deciding the present case by determining what was done in a prior similar case—literally "the thing decided").

An additional method of analysis was undertaken by Blackstone. Assuming that a custom or common law exists, the next step would be to inquire as to the legality of it; if it is not a good custom, it should not be allowed to survive. To make a custom "good" under the common law, seven requirements must be met:

1. It has been used so long that no one can remember a custom to the contrary.

2. Its use has been continuous and uninterrupted.
3. It has been peaceable and accepted—it is not subject to confusion and dispute.
4&5. It must be reasonable and certain.
6. The use of the custom must be compulsory for all people.
7. The custom must be consistent with other customs.[24]

Since Blackstone, the appellate courts of England and America have been the basic depositories of the common law. The various appeal level cases have determined what the unwritten common law is. In America, when the colonies were first established, the common law was deemed to be the law of the land. As the various states exercised their independence after 1776, statutes were enacted superseding the common law on almost every conceivable subject. Presently no state exists on common law alone. The states have all attempted to make statutory law all-encompassing. Such a condition does not, however, mean that the common law is dead.

The common law still has a great deal of importance in at least two circumstances:

1) If there is a gap in statutory law some condition which is not covered—the courts may refer to the common law to resolve the dispute.[25]
2) Statutes are to be read in the light of the common law, and a statute affirming a common-law rule is to be construed in ac-

> cordance with the common law.[26] The common law must however give way to any statute which is inconsistent with it.[27]

Many states have by statute provided that the common law of England, so far as it is not repugnant to or inconsistent with the Constitution of the United States or the constitution or laws of the state, is the rule governing decisions in that state.[28]

THE CONCEPT OF *STARE DECISIS*

Against the background of the common-law tradition, the concept of *stare decisis* stands out as the primary tool by which the common law grew, developed, and changed. It is also the tool by which statutory interpretation takes place. *Stare decisis* means: "to abide by, or adhere to, decided cases."[29] The original longer version was: *stare decisis et non quieta movere,* which means "to adhere to precedents and not to unsettle things which are established."[30]

Blackstone described the process as one where the older case was examined in order to find if the same points were once again being questioned; if such was the case, Blackstone declared it to be an established rule to abide by former precedents. He noted that this would keep the scales of justice even and steady and would not allow them to waver with each new judge who came along. The doctrine for Blackstone was that precedents and rules must be followed unless a court found them to be obviously absurd or unjust. If such a finding were made, the court would not say it was a bad law, but rather would say it *never was the law*—that it was earlier incorrectly determined to be the law.[31]

Volumes have been written on the subject of *stare decisis*, analyzing and describing the methods by which the law changes over the years. Many factors enter into the process and influence the decisions. The record of proceedings in the trial court is always important, for the trial lawyers may have left certain things out and included others, any of which may turn out to be the deciding factor. The lawyer presenting the case on appeal will emphasize in the record those facts which are similar to the facts described in precedent cases. Because any two cases will very seldom contain exactly the same facts, the lawyer as a craftsman must carefully select the precedent cases he will use in order to find those that will help him the most. He must, in cases which go against him, also point out the facts which distinguish that case from the present case to be decided. Without changing the facts of his own case, he must shape and mold these facts into the best possible presentation.

Some confusion always exists as to how any predictability can ever be brought into our system of law. The law changes and precedent changes—how can a citizen ever depend on the outcome? Our system has always been one in which we view precedent as welcome and persuasive, but we do not hesitate to change the law if we feel it to be unjust.

Karl Llewelyn provided some of the answers to these questions. He described the "grand style of the common law" as a manner of thought and work, not a style of writing. The constant re-examination and reworking of the heritage of law, the reasoning, testing, and shaping of various legal principles is a constant and never-ending process in the appeals courts.[32] Opinions of appeals courts, to those who watch, read, and understand the process, provide a clear insight into what the law is now and where it is heading. Written opinions keep judges within certain bounds. When writing an opinion, a judge must anticipate future cases not yet before him, and he will thus be determining how like cases are to be decided in the future. The opinion is a steadying factor, which aids in predictability because it forces a court to look backward at other cases as well as forward to its effect on new cases.[33]

In deciding whether to apply a particular precedent case, many courts will apply three tests:

> 1. What is the reputation of the judge and the court which produced the opinion in question; 2, Does the theory set forth fit with established principle; and 3, Is the opinion reasonable in light of public policy considerations.[34]

Others describe the process in terms of legal reasoning—reasoning by example and reasoning from case to case. The logical steps are these: similarity is seen between two cases; next, the rule of law from the first case is determined; then the rule of law is applied to the second case.[35]

Examples, analogies, and writings of experts are introduced into the system by the parties before the court. The ideas and desires of society also enter into the process. A concept may be suggested in one case and win no approval by the court; later, the concept may become important to society and a later court may adopt it.[36]

Certain theories and ideas that are not strictly necessary are presented in many opinions. Such a portion of a legal opinion is termed *dictum*, and as such it does not receive the same respect as a strict holding. Courts find it easier to rule contrary to *dictum* than to a holding.

Reasoning by example means that lawyers will point out the differences as well as the similarities that precedent cases have to the case in question. Out of the mixture of competing examples, the court must then come up with the most reasonable answer in light of the prior cases. Reasoning by example is used in the interpretation of case law, statutes, and the Constitution. Ambiguity is always going to be present in statutes, thus an interpretation allows shading and shaping of a legislative concept. Legislation, however, binds a court's future decisions much more than case law, particularly since courts must give weight to the intent of the legislature.

CONSTITUTIONAL PROVISIONS

The Constitution of the United States has been interpreted in such a way as to give the courts power to invalidate legislative acts.[37] Any statute must fall within the confines of the Constitution; if a conflict becomes apparent, the statute falls, whether it is a federal or a state statute. For example, a federal statute once existed that laid out a presumption that marijuana in one's possession had come across international boundaries. In the Leary case, the defendant was arrested with a quantity of marijuana and charged with a violation of the Marijuana Tax Stamp Act for failure to pay the appropriate border tax. Timothy Leary's federal conviction for possession of marijuana was overturned because such a presumption had no basis in fact and reason and thus could not be squared with the Fifth and Fourteenth Amendments to the United States Constitution requiring that an individual be given "due process of law."[38] Example: A statute making it a crime to commit an act which "outrages public decency," is unconstitutionally vague. When an act is forbidden in terms so vague that a person of ordinary intelligence cannot interpret the scope intended and must only guess at its meaning, the act violates due process of law. A person is never required to speculate as to the meaning of a penal statute.[39]

The United States Constitution and Bill of Rights were written after the revolt against the arbitrary measures of King George III. Feelings were strong that government should be restricted and controlled, partly because of what England had done and partly because of the philosophy of the French Revolution. The drafters of the Constitution placed "the maximum restrictions upon the power of organized society over the individual that are compatible with the maintenance of organized society itself. [Constitutional provisions] were so intended and should be so interpreted. It cannot be denied that, even if construed as their provisions traditionally have been, they contain an aggregate of restrictions which seriously limit the power of society to solve . . . crimes."[40] That limitation on the power to solve crimes simply must be accepted as the lesser of two evils; an oppressive, overpowerful government would be worse. Justice Felix Frankfurter of the U. S. Supreme Court set forth the reason succinctly: "The history of liberty has largely been the history of observance of procedural safeguards."[41]

As may be seen, the courts, through case law and the Constitution, exercise an important check upon the powers of the legislative and executive branches of government, including administration of justice personnel. Were it not for the courts (and the Constitution), a powerful governor, in cooperation with the state legislature, could enact legislation or executive order declaring that the police may search any person on a hunch or may stop and search every car on a public highway in order to find marijuana. This, of course, is all part of our systems of "checks and balances" wherein one branch of government serves to check the power of the other. The basic, most important and most common constitutional restrictions on the power of Congress and legislatures are these:

1. *The First Amendment.* The First Amendment prohibits a state from making it a crime to sell pornography unless a proper definition of what is obscene is spelled out. Merely to say it is "obscene" is not enough—it must be material that taken as a whole, and applying contemporary standards, has a predominant appeal to prurient interests in sex, nudity, or excretion; is material that goes substantially beyond the customary limits of candor in the community; and is material utterly without redeeming social importance.[42] If a statute prohibits the sale of something that is not obscene, the statute must fall and be useless.

Also, under the First Amendment "free speech"

provisions, persons are protected from state restrictions when they peaceably assemble, protest, and move about. As a result, the courts have taken rather harsh attitudes toward vagrancy statutes. The basic problem is that in a free society law enforcement agencies are not to have unbounded authority to arrest anyone they wish for "vagrancy" merely because of his status, appearance, or presence in a particular place. Courts have required that some act of violence or other act affecting the rights of others be committed before arrest and criminal sanctions are imposed. To do otherwise would allow too much risk of arbitrary law enforcement.[43]

In reading the Bill of Rights—the first ten amendments to the United States Constitution—one notes that they provide restriction only on the acts of Congress. How then has the Bill of Rights been interpreted to be a restriction on state legislative action? The answer is that under the Fourteenth Amendment appear these words: "Nor shall *any state* deprive any persons of life, liberty, or property, without due process of law" (emphasis added). "Due process," to the United States Supreme Court, has come to mean most (but not all) of those rights as set forth in the first ten amendments. States must properly define obscenity, not because the state is required to do so by the First Amendment, but rather because the state is required to exercise "due process of law." "Due process" means that a state must have a proper definition for obscenity, and a proper definition happens to be that which is used in regulating the federal government under the First Amendment. Although the Fourteenth Amendment has not been interpreted to mean that all the amendments of the Bill of Rights apply to the states, all major parts have been incorporated, thus limiting state action in almost the same areas as federal action is limited. Basically, it is those rights which are "fundamental" to our system of justice and "implicit in the concept of ordered liberty" that are used to control state actions[44] in the same way that federal action is limited, only fundamental rights are considered to be included in the "due process" of the Fourteenth Amendment.

2. *Search and Seizure Rules.* Under the Fourth Amendment (and the Fourteenth), the state and federal governments must respect a person's right to be free from all but reasonable searches, i.e., those which are based upon a warrant or upon reasonable and probable cause.[45] Only unreasonable searches are prohibited. A massive body of case law has developed defining the types of search that governmental officials may and may not make.

The Fourth Amendment has raised a critical question regarding methods of enforcement. Originally, a civil lawsuit requesting a dollar award could be filed against a police officer who violated the Fourth Amendment. But in 1914, an "exclusionary rule" was developed in federal cases. This rule required that evidence be suppressed and kept out of court when the evidence was obtained by way of an illegal search.[46] However, states could still convict people by use of unlawfully seized evidence until 1961, when the United States Supreme Court interpreted the Fourth and Fourteenth Amendments as prohibiting the use of such evidence in a state prosecution.[47] "...[T]he purpose of the exclusionary rule 'is to deter—to compel respect for the constitutional guaranty in the only effective available way—by removing the incentive to disregard it.' "[48] To allow unlawfully seized evidence to be admitted would be to encourage disobedience of the Constitution.[49]

3. *The Fifth Amendment.* Under the Fifth Amendment for capital or infamous crimes, a "screening process" must be held to "weed out" bad cases and bad charges. No one should be required to go through the inconvenience, expense, and worries of a trial when there is no case against him. Thus, for any felony, either a grand jury indictment or a preliminary hearing before a magistrate is required.[50] Once a strong suspicion has been shown, either by grand jury process or by preliminary hearing process, the state may order a person to trial.

4. *Double Jeopardy.* Also under the Fifth Amendment, no person may be tried twice for the same offense.

5. *Self-incrimination.* The most widely recognized right is the right not to incriminate one's self, as set forth in the Fifth Amendment. Under the exclusionary rule, illegal searches, confessions obtained by improper pressures, and confessions that are forced from a person are excluded from evidence. The self-incrimination privilege has always been considered to be closely related to the right to counsel provisions spelled out in the Sixth Amendment. If a lawyer is engaged, before questioning he will almost certainly (and properly) advise his client to remain silent.

In determining whether or not a confession is admissible, courts must decide whether or not the statement was freely and voluntarily given. Such a determination depends upon what types of advisements were made to the suspect by the police, how long he had been in custody, whether or not he was in custody, whether or not he was properly arrested, and many other factors.[51]

6. *Speedy Trial.* A person cannot be held for long periods of time awaiting trial. The Sixth Amendment prohibits unreasonable delays, and cases have been dismissed for this reason, especially if the delay caused prejudice against the defendant (such as the death of a defense witness during the delay). The right is a fundamental one and is incorporated into the Fourteenth Amendment, thus applicable to the states.[52]

7. *Jury Trial.* All persons accused of a crime are guaranteed under the Sixth Amendment a jury trial if they desire one. Jury trials are fundamental to the American system of justice, and are also provided for under the Fourteenth Amendment. The jury has been considered as a means of protection for the individual against arbitrary rule and oppression by the government. It further protects against judges who are too responsive to the voice of higher authority.[53] Persons accused of minor crimes that do not carry jail penalties, such as parking violations and minor traffic violations, do not have the right to a jury trial.

8. *Confrontation of the Accuser.* A person charged with a crime has a fundamental right under the Sixth and Fourteenth Amendments to see the people who testify against him and also to have them cross-examined.[54] Such a requirement means that written statements or depositions (even though in affidavit form) cannot be used in court, except in very unusual circumstances.

9. *The Right to Counsel.* Under the Sixth and Fourteenth Amendments, all persons accused of a crime have the right to have an attorney, and if no

funds are available to pay a fee, the state must provide the accused persons with a competent lawyer.[55] An attorney is just as necessary for a guilty person as for an innocent person. For an innocent person, the attorney must try to gain an acquittal. For the person who acknowledges guilt, the attorney has two basic functions:

1. To bring all possible mitigating factors before the sentencing judge in order to obtain the most appropriate sentence.
2. To be sure the charges are in the proper degree before a guilty plea is entered. Often a case is filed as a murder when it really should be a manslaughter; the attorney should then attempt to push the case is that direction.

Understanding the functions answers the questions often asked by laymen of attorneys, "How can you justify defending a guilty person?"

Other rights exist under the federal and various state constitutions; all are meant to be a means of restricting, in the criminal context, the powers of the state. Some of the fundamental rights spelled out above do not apply to children in juvenile court who are accused of crimes. The rationale has been that children are not convicted of crimes, rather they are declared wards of the court and are sometimes taken from their parents. By making the hearing an action to merely replace the parents with a court, in a civil action rather than a criminal action, denial of some of the criminal constitutional rights may be justified. The cases involving juveniles carry penalties, however, and constitutional requirements must be observed, at least in part.

Before 1967, few constitutional rights were afforded to juveniles. In that year, the United States Supreme Court, in the *Gault* v. *Arizona* case,[56] declared that the "civil" label placed on juvenile proceedings was "mere rhetoric." The thought that the juvenile process was "rehabilitative" and "clinical" rather than punitive simply did not give a state the right to ignore constitutional requirements. The Court said, "Juvenile court history has again demonstrated that unbridled discretion, however benevolently motivated, is frequently a poor substitute for principle and procedure." Thus, under due process of law as defined in *Gault*, juvenile courts must do the following in any case where confinement in an institution may come about:

1. Present the accused with proper notice—a clear and specific statement of charges.
2. Advise the minor and his parents of their right to have an attorney and if they are unable to afford an attorney, that the court will appoint one for them.
3. Concurrently with the right to counsel, the court must also advise the minor of his privilege against self-incrimination and that he cannot be required to make any statement against his own interests.
4. Abide by the person's right to confront and cross-examine witnesses against him.

Since *Gault*, the Supreme Court has also held that no longer can a determination of wardship be based on a *preponderance of evidence;* rather, the adult standard *guilt beyond a reasonable doubt* must be used before a juvenile can be convicted.[57]

One notable fundamental right afforded to adults is still denied to children—the right to a jury trial. It remains to be seen whether or not the Supreme Court will eventually grant this right to children.

PRE-EMPTION

The problem of pre-emption arises when the laws of two government entities conflict, particularly when an act is legal under one and illegal under the other. Generally, it can be said that when such a situation develops, the higher government entity prevails over the lower.

Under pre-emption theories, a city or county cannot attempt to make theft a violation of county or city ordinance for the reason that the state has already occupied the field by making theft a violation of the state penal code. Once the state proceeds to regulate a particular, well-defined area, no lesser government entity will be allowed to make decisions in that same field.

REPEAL

Statutes, penal and otherwise, may be repealed and eliminated from the books. As times change, the requirements of society change, and acts once prohibited may be allowed. A few states, for example, have repealed statutes prohibiting homosexual acts between consenting adults.

Statutes may be repealed by an act of the state legislature and also, in many states, by a referendum—a vote of the people. A referendum may be initiated by obtaining the required number of signatures on a petition. Once the petition is properly filed, the referendum will appear on the ballot for a vote. Such a procedure provides the citizen with a method for taking action when the state legislature becomes non-responsive to his desires and needs.

MALA-IN-SE VERSUS MALA-PROHIBITA CRIMES

As noted earlier in this chapter, throughout history, people dealing with the law have distinguished between *mala in se* and *mala prohibita* crimes. The former concerns those acts which are bad in and of themselves (generally, murder, assault, rape, etc.); the latter involves acts which are bad only because a governing body has declared them prohibited (generally, bigamy, homosexual acts by adults, etc.). The distinction, however, seldom serves any useful function, except that if a statute is clearly *mala in se* in origin, it is given more serious attention and is not so likely to be altered or repealed.

CRIMES WITHOUT VICTIMS

Often crimes without victims (public drunkenness, possession of marijuana, prostitution, bookmaking, etc.) are pointed out as being illustrative of crimes that could well be eliminated from the books so that more time and money could be devoted to the prosecution of "real" crimes, such as murder and robbery. As crime statistics rise, budgetary demands from police and prosecution agencies also rise. Many authorities believe that eventually, certain crimes will have to be forgotten. The "victimless" crimes could be the first to go.

By one interpretation, there is no such thing as a "victimless" crime. When a person uses drugs that damage his brain and make him nonproductive, he is a victim and so is society in general, for it is society that may have to support him through welfare payments. In making decisions to repeal or decline prosecution, each crime must be examined individually in light of present circumstances. Clearly, there should be more inducement to arrest and prosecute a person for possessing LSD as opposed to one who engages in bookmaking.

POLICE POWER

The local police, prosecuting agencies, and others making up the administration of justice derive their power to act from the state constitutions. The United States government obtains its power to act from the specific grants of power in the main body of the United States Constitution, specifically:

1. Power to regulate commerce among the several states (thus, the federal crime of interstate transportation of stolen vehicles)[58]

2. Power to punish counterfeiting violations[59]
3. Power to make all laws necessary and proper for carrying into execution the various other powers of government of the United States (thus, the crime of conspiracies to obstruct justice)[60]
4. Power to declare treason a crime[61]

Since no mention of common-law crimes is made in the United States Constitution, the Tenth Amendment by implication gives the states the power to regulate and define crimes such as murder and theft. The Tenth Amendment states: "The powers not delegated to the United States by the Constitution, nor prohibited by it to the states, are reserved to the states respectively, or to the people."[62] In sum, the federal government can act only under specific grants of power; the states cover everything else.

SUBSTANTIVE VERSUS PROCEDURAL LAW

The distinction between substantive and procedural law does not serve to resolve many issues, although it does sometimes serve as a vehicle for analysis. Earlier in this chapter, various procedural law requirements under the Bill of Rights were set forth; these provisions for due process were intended to secure the individual from the arbitrary exercise of the powers of government.[63] This is the ultimate function and object of procedural law.

Interpretations of substantive law became more difficult to identify and classify. Examples of substantive law are: a speed limit on highways, obscenity laws, etc. Substantive law deals with the desires and wants of various individuals that may be inconsistent with the desires and wants of other individuals. Substantive may be that which is not procedural.[64]

At any rate, determining whether an issue involves substantive or procedural law does not assist in resolving the issue. The issue must be decided on the basis of the Constitution, case law, appropriate statutes, and public policy whether it is substantive or procedural in nature.

Endnotes

1. Roscoe Pound, *An Introduction to the Philosophy of Law*, (Colonial Press Inc., 1921, 1954) p. 2.
2. Ibid., p. 4.
3. Ibid., p. 6.
4. Ibid., p. 34.
5. Ibid., p. 35.
6. Ibid., p. 8.
7. Ibid., p. 9.
8. Ibid., p. 10.
9. Ibid., p. 11.
10. Ibid., p. 12.
11. Ibid., p. 36.
12. Ibid., pp. 13, 37.

13. Ibid., pp. 16–17, 37.
14. Ibid., pp. 18–19.
15. James F. Stephen, *History of the Criminal Law of England*, (1883) Vol. 2, p. 94.
16. Ibid., pp. 94–95. See also: infra Chapter 5.
17. Ibid., pp. 124–26, p. 183; Daniel M'Naghten's Case, 4 St. TR. N.S. 847, 8 Eng. Rep. 718 (1843).
18. Jeremy Bentham, *A Treatise on Judicial Evidence*, (1825) pp. 196–98.
19. William Blackstone, *Commentaries on the Laws of England* Vol. 1 (Oxford: Clarendon Press, 1765; reprinted by Dawsons of Pall Mall, London, 1966), p. 63.
20. Ibid., p. 64.
21. Ibid., p. 67.
22. Ibid., p. 68.
23. Ibid., p. 69.
24. Ibid., pp. 76–78.
25. Fletcher v. Los Angeles Trust etc. Bank, 182 Cal. 177 (1920).
26. Bandfield v. Bandfield, 117 Mich 80.
27. Hamilton v. Rathbone, 175 U.S. 414.
28. Fletcher v. Los Angeles Trust etc. Bank, p. 182; Calif. Civil Code, Section 22.2.
29. *Black's Law Dictionary*, 4th ed. rev., West Publishing Co., 1968. St Paul, Minn.
30. Ibid.
31. Blackstone, *Commentaries on the Laws of England*, p. 70.
32. Karl N. Llewelyn, *The Common Law Tradition* (Boston: Little, Brown & Co., 1960), p. 36.
33. Ibid., p. 26.

34. Ibid., p. 36.
35. Edward H. Levi, *An Introduction to Legal Reasoning* (Chicago: University of Chicago Press, 1948) pp. 1–2.
36. Ibid., p. 5.
37. Marbury v. Madison, 1 Cr. U.S. 137 (1803).
38. Leary v. United States, 395 U.S. 6 (1969).
39. In re Davis, 242 Cal. App. 2d. 645 (1966).
40. Watts v. Indiana, 338 U.S. 49, 61 (1949).
41. McNabb v. United States, 318 U.S. 332, 347 (1943).
42. In re Giannini, 395 U.S. 910 (1968); Ginsberg v. New York, 390 U.S. 629 (1968).
43. Aptheker v. Secretary of State, 378 U.S. 500, 520 (1964); Shuttlesworth v. Birmingham, 382 U.S. 87 (1965).
44. Palko v. Connecticut, 302 U.S. 317 (1937).
45. Mapp v. Ohio, 367 U.S. 643 (1961).
46. Weeks v. United States, 232 U.S. 383 (1914).
47. Mapp v. Ohio, 367 U.S. 643 (1961).
48. Ibid., p. 656.
49. Ibid., p. 657.
50. Hurtado v. California, 110 U.S. 516 (1884).
51. McNabb v. United States, 318 U.S. 332 (1943); Miranda v. Arizona, 384 U.S. 436 (1966).
52. Klopfer v. State of North Carolina, 386 U.S. 213 (1967).
53. Duncan v. State of Louisiana, 391 U.S. 146, 155 (1968).
54. Pointer v. Texas, 380 U.S. 400 (1965).
55. Gideon v. Wainwright, 372 U.S. 335 (1963).
56. In re Gault, 387 U.S. 1 (1967).

57. Winship v. New York, 394 U.S. 358 (1969).
58. United States Constitution, Article I, Section 8.
59. Ibid.
60. Ibid.
61. United States Constitution, Article III, Section 3.
62. United States Constitution, Tenth Amendment.
63. Twining v. New Jersey, 211 U.S. 78 (1908).
64. Freund, Sutherland, Howe, and Brown, *II Constitutional Law,* (Boston: Little, Brown & Co., 1961), p. 1027.

QUESTIONS

1. Relate the needs that can be seen as controlling forces behind philosophical thinking in the area of law.
2. Review the development of law in the following civilizations: Babylonian, Egyptian, Hebrew, Greek, and Roman.
3. Describe the historical background of common law.
4. Name seven requirements that satisfy the creation of a custom under common law.
5. Define *stare decisis* and describe its ramifications upon the interpretation of the law.
6. What effect does the interpretation of the U.S. Constitution have upon criminal statutes?
7. Review the constitutional rights afforded by the

First, Fourth, Fifth, Sixth, and Fourteenth Amendments to the U.S. Constitution.

8. Relate the constitutional provisions afforded juveniles and discuss the case decision that is responsible for this departure.
9. What effect do pre-emption and repeal have upon the law?
10. Explain the difference between *mala in se* crime and *mala prohibita* crime.
11. Trace the sources of police power and enumerate the powers granted to the states.

Chapter Three

THE NATURE OF CRIMINAL LAW

THE DEFINITION OF CRIME

Crime over the years has had many definitions ranging from the simplest: that a crime is a public offense against the state, to a more complicated statement that defines crime as a course of conduct or practice that is detrimental to public welfare and that is prohibited. Crime can further be defined as an act committed or omitted in violation of a law forbidding or commanding it and to which is annexed, upon conviction, certain penalties.

Presently, the United States and most of the states do not recognize the common law as such, although most state penal codes are based in large part on the common law. Since all public offenses or crimes are statutory, the courts cannot now have recourse to common law to determine prohibited acts. Certain criteria must be present before a crime can be valid: 1) the crime must be enacted by a legislature; 2) the crime must be published for all to see; 3) the crime must be specifically defined, not indefinite or vague; 4) the statute must prescribe a punishment of some type; and 5) from a philosophical point of view, the crime must be uniformly enforced.

Joel Prentis Bishop defined crime in terms of the "wrong done." He declares: "A crime is any wrong which the government deems injurious to the public at large and punishes through a judicial proceeding in its own name."[1] In defining crime, Rollin M. Perkins said, "A crime is any social harm defined and made punishable by law."[2]

THE PURPOSE OF CRIMINAL LAW

The law is currently used to identify that institution of social control that attempts to prevent crime and disorder and preserve the peace and that attempts to protect the life, property, and personal liberty of the individual.

The specific role of criminal law has neither been clearly defined nor accepted by practitioners and academicians. Many individuals have narrow views of the criminal law and identify it with the limited function of crime repression and suppression—the mechanical treadmill of investigation, identification, apprehension, and prosecution. Many individuals have felt recently that the role should be expanded to include crime prevention activities and awareness of the conditions of social welfare causing crime. Many communities feel that the criminal law exists to purify people—a commendable goal, but not the proper function of the law. Others feel the criminal law should protect the neighborhood from one who questions the status quo. Such a desire is most unreasonable.

In so far as serious crimes are concerned there is broad disagreement among the world's many criminal law systems regarding what behavior to punish.

Though somewhat differently defined in various areas, the *mala in se* crimes (i.e., murder, rape, robbery, arson, theft, assault, etc.) form the common staple of serious crime. But there the agreement stops; great divergence is to be found among legal systems on what further behavior should fall under the prohibitions of criminal law.

The use of the threat and the actuality of criminal punishments to attempt to coerce men to follow a good and moral life seem to be a gross overreach of the criminal law. It is argued that in seeking to enforce such acts as "victimless crimes" (i.e., drunkenness, drug abuse, gambling, disorderly conduct, vagrancy, homosexuality, prostitution, etc.), the criminal law is not only ineffective and wasteful, but also injures rather than protects the community.

Consequently, whether the act is a so-called victimless crime or an act that is wrong in and of itself, the role of the criminal law means a variety of things to a variety of people. Some of the expressed purposes of the law include the desire: 1) for vengeance; 2) to prevent public injury; 3) to protect life and property; 4) to serve as punishment; 5) to define conduct; 6) to compel people to refrain from committing crimes; 7) to force people into the conformance of established rules.

THE LANGUAGE AND CONSTRUCTION OF PENAL STATUTES

The construction and language of penal statutes can become important in the interpretation, application, and enforcement of prohibited acts.

If a statute is so vague and lacking in ascertainable standards of guilt that it fails to give a "person of ordinary intelligence fair notice that his contemplated conduct is forbidden" the statute is unconstitutional.[3] The underlying principle is that no man shall be held criminally responsible for conduct that he could not reasonably understand to be prescribed.[4]

For example, a city ordinance once made it an offense for three or more persons to assemble on any of the sidewalks and conduct themselves in a manner annoying to persons passing by. The Supreme Court held it unconstitutional on its face for vagueness because it provided no standard by which one could determine what conduct constitutes an annoyance.[5] Criminal statutes that are vague and uncertain constitute a violation of the due process clause of the Fourteenth Amendment to the United States Constitution and cannot be enforced.[6]

The rule of thumb in construing penal statutes is that criminal statutes are not to be strictly construed, but rather should be interpreted so as to promote fairness and justice. When construing penal statutes, one must take into consideration the "spirit of the law, not the letter of the law." Although penal statutes cannot be vague and indefinite, many are flexible and can be "stretched" to fit a particular situation. An example of this is the dangerous weapons-control law enacted by many states to classify certain weapons as contraband and to prohibit the possession of these weapons. Weapons prohibited by the statutes include: brass knuckles, billy clubs, dirks, etc. Tape wrapped around one's knuckles has been construed as brass knuckles; tire irons and baseball bats have been construed as billy clubs; a chisel that was sharpened on both sides and that came to a point has been construed as being a dirk.[7] Any motorist who carries a tire iron in his car to fix his flat tire could be considered to be breaking the law if a police officer construed the tire iron to be a billy club and thus interpreted the law. Fortunately, police officers have broad discretionary powers, and this discretion lends itself well to the spirit of the law.

It is this same police discretion that enables a police officer to conclude that a crime has been committed, but that it is not beneficial to the community to pursue the prosecution. For example, if a drunk is standing on the sidewalk in front of his own home and has not been driving, many police officers may release him to his home rather than arrest him. Such a course of action is often encouraged in situations where rather extensive costs would come about by pursuing a prosecution.

CONFLICTS BETWEEN STATUTES

One can find examples where a particular type of conduct is prohibited by more than one statute. For instance, it is a theft to make false representations to the welfare department for purposes of obtaining welfare money. Such an act is also often prohibited by a specific statute dealing with welfare fraud. When the theft is a felony, and the welfare fraud is a misdemeanor, such a distinction becomes drastically important to the accused.

To resolve the question of which statute to apply, a legal theory has developed holding that the specific statute controls the general statute. The state legislature, so the reasoning goes, has examined this particular specific situation and has determined that a more particularized statute is necessary and proper; thus, by implication, the general statute (theft, in the example above) is repealed or declared inoperative in some circumstances. Such an interpretation is based on the rule of law that criminal statutes are to be interpreted liberally in favor of the accused. Other examples of the specific statutes as opposed to general statutes are those regarding receiving stolen property, which is a felony as opposed to possession of a stolen credit card; forgery as opposed to the misdemeanor of using someone's credit card; theft as opposed to the misdemeanor crime of making false statements to an insurance company to collect a claim.

If two statutes conflict in more dramatic fashion, the latter statute controls over the earlier. By implication, the state legislature has repealed the earlier one in that situation.

THE DISTINCTION BETWEEN CRIMES AND TORTS

	Crime	Tort
1.	Public wrong	Private wrong
2.	State prosecutes	Individual prosecutes
3.	Seeks to punish	Seeks redress for injury
4.	Criminal intent is required	Intent not necessary

When one person is assaulted by another, technically the victim can request that the state punish the defendant by convicting him criminally; in addition, he may require compensation from the defendant for any injuries sustained. It is ironic that in a criminal prosecution, even though the victim is the person who sustains the injury, he technically is not the one who prosecutes. Under the criminal law, the victim is the state—not the person who sustained the injury. However, if the victim who sustains the injury sues civilly for any damages accumulated because of the injury, the victim is the injured party and is the one who pursues the action.

Neither the criminal proceeding nor the civil proceeding is a bar to the other; therefore, the concept of double jeopardy does not pertain. However, if the defendant pleads *nolo contendere* (no contest) in the criminal trial (which is in effect a guilty plea), the plea cannot be used against him in any subsequent civil proceeding for the same case.

While the function of the criminal proceeding is to punish the defendant in the form of either fine, jail, imprisonment, or death, the civil proceeding serves to compensate the victim in the following areas. If an injury has been incurred through stupidity or negligence, the plaintiff may recover "general" damages such as medical bills, drugs, prescriptions, loss of earnings, and loss of earning capacity. Also, "special" damages can be recovered for the amount of pain incurred. If the defendant's actions were deliberate or intentional, "punitive" (or "exemplary") damages may be recovered in order to punish the defendant and to serve as a deterrent for any future action. An example of this is assault and battery.

CRIMINAL AND CIVIL LIABILITY

Because of congressional enactments, the United States Department of Justice maintains an interest in the conduct of criminal justice participants. The federal government may bring a criminal prosecution against a member of the criminal justice system for violation of civil rights, and often this occurrence tends to strain the everyday relationship between federal, local, and state officials. The participant involved, his professional association, and some of the public who learns of the matter through newspaper accounts frequently react with a feeling of deep resentment.

What gives the federal government the right to interfere? Why should some bureaucrat in Washington sit in judgment over members of the criminal justice system who are dedicated to upholding the law?

The supreme law of the land is the United States Constitution. It sets up a system of federalism allocating most of the authority to states and local authorities. The states in turn allocate it to counties and cities in accordance with state constitutions and laws. The authority granted to the states by the United States Constitution is subject to some restrictions and is not absolute. Certain individual rights are so important as to be guaranteed by the constitution and are conferred directly to individuals.

The Fourteenth Amendment purports to restrict the power and authority of the states. Speaking in terms of a state's actions, the Fourteenth Amendment provides that no state shall deprive its citizens of life, liberty, or property without due process of law and that no citizen shall be denied equal protection of the law. The Amendment also grants Congress the right to implement that Amendment and give it teeth by passing supporting legislation. A state resembles a corporation in the sense that the only way it can act is through its agents and through its officials. For the state to actually deprive a citizen of life, liberty, or property or any other constitutional and guaranteed right without due process violates the Fourteenth Amendment.

One of the implementing statutes under the Fourteenth Amendment is Title 18, United States Code, section 242, which reads: "whoever under color of any law, statute, ordinance, regulation or custom willfully subjects any inhabitant of any state, territory or district to the deprivation of any rights, privileges or immunities secured or protected by the constitution, or laws of the United States, shall be fined not more than one thousand dollars or imprisoned not more than one year, or both; and (by a 1968 amendment) if death results, shall be subject to imprisonment for any term the court orders or for any year or determinant years or for life." Over the years this statute has received varying interpretations and has been interpreted differently by the various courts. In one of the classic cases under this section, a sheriff released a prisoner to a lynch mob that mistreated him and ultimately killed him; the sheriff was prosecuted under this section, and it was held by the court of appeal that the sheriff had violated the section by depriving the victim of the opportunity for a trial under due process of law. By turning the prisoner over to the mob, he had prevented the man, guilty or not, from receiving a fair trial.

The judicial and congressional attempts to eliminate summary punishment by criminal justice authorities run throughout the federal law. An accused person has the federal right to be tried and if he is found guilty, then punished. The courts reason that if an official intentionally strikes a person on his head with the intent not of applying reasonable force to effect the arrest but to punish the man on the spot for what he did, he is depriving the man of the right to a trial and therefore depriving him of a federal constitutional right. If a criminal justice official were to go across a state line to capture a fugitive without a warrant, the official is depriving the fugitive of the right to contest the extradition and therefore is depriving the fugitive of due process of the law. If the official makes a false arrest, in theory he does not have enough probable cause to make an arrest and could be considered for prosecution under this section. Because section 242 is so broad, the Department of Justice has developed through the years a series of guidelines or criteria for the investigation and prosecution of these offenses.

After a complaint has been received by the Justice Department from the Federal Bureau of Investigation, a "preliminary investigation" is conducted. The role of the Justice Department is to collect and evaluate the basic facts and to sort out the cases that should be prosecuted from the cases that are instigated for improper reasons, such as those that attempt to set up a defense to a state charge, those that try to undermine public faith in law enforcement, and those that attempt to search for facts to reverse a conviction. In a preliminary investigation, the complainant is interviewed regarding details of the alleged offense, and the relevant criminal justice records are obtained. The interviews and reports gathered are sent to Washington and to a United States Attorney working in the Justice Department. After review and discussion, it is estimated that between 75 and 80 percent of the cases are closed after the preliminary investigation.

The Civil Rights Division of the Department of Justice has approximately 106 attorneys, of whom 12 work on evaluating criminal cases. More than 3000 cases were investigated in a recent one-year period, and 33 criminal justice participants were charged with violations of a civil rights act.[8]

Concerning civil liability, each state has its own set of laws, public avenues of civil liability against members of the criminal justice system. Because these statutes are so varied, California's system will be described as a model.

"The comprehensive scheme of tort legislation" applies to every public entity (such as a city) within the state of California and provides that if the criminal justice employee were acting within the course and scope of his employment at the time of the alleged civil violation, his place of employment must represent him. If they do not, they must pay for the ensuing civil suit if there is an adverse judgment. The employing entity must indemnify the employee for general and special damages; because of section 818 of the Government Code, the public entity is not required to pay punitive damages.

Generally, law suits concerning tort liability fall into two categories: intentional torts and unintentional torts (negligence). The most common intentional torts include false arrest, false imprisonment, assault and battery under color of authority without due process of law, or wrongful death where there is a violation of civil rights. If a criminal justice employee commits an intentional tort, not only is he liable for his intentional action but, if he is acting in the course and scope of his employment, so is his employing entity. This is called the doctrine of *respondeat superior,* which allows a plaintiff to sue not only the employee but also his employing entity. The tort of false arrest arises out of an unlawful assertion of police authority over a person, resulting in a restraint on his liberty. False arrest is said to be the same as false imprisonment, and often they are treated as one cause of action. A person who is wrongfully arrested is also wrongfully imprisoned. However, a person wrongfully imprisoned may not have been wrongfully arrested. The actions differ in two significant particulars: 1) A private individual can commit an act of false imprisonment without an arrest. 2) A person legally arrested can thereafter be falsely imprisoned when there has been an unreasonable delay in taking him before a magistrate or where he has been detained after he has a right to be released.

The essential elements of a tort action of false arrest include: 1) the confinement of the plaintiff, 2) within boundaries fixed by the defendant, 3) an arrest without legal justification and, 4) an arrest by an act or breach of a duty intended to result in such confinement. The key to the action is whether or not the criminal justice employee acted lawfully in making the arrest. An arrest is an actual restraint of a person or his involuntary submission to the custody of an officer. Even a momentarily taking an individual into custody is an arrest. The plaintiff must, however, be conscious that he has been arrested, and his submission must be against his will.

An officer who properly carries out the directive of a valid arrest warrant will not be liable for false arrest. However, statistics reveal that the overwhelming majority of arrests are made without warrants. The following example serves to identify a situation in which there is both a false arrest and false imprisonment. An adult male, walking at 3:00 A.M. in an industrial area with a high burglary rate, is observed by a police officer. The police officer has an obligation and is legally justified in making reasonable inquiries as to the identity of the individual and as to his reason for being in the neighborhood. The individual properly identifies himself and relates that he is just out for a walk. However, he refuses to answer any further questions presented to him by the officer. Keeping in mind the high burglary rate district, the hour of the night, and the refusal of the individual to answer any further questions, the officer arrests the person for suspicion of burglary and removes him to a police department for further investigation. Based upon the above facts, the officer has committed a false arrest and false imprisonment. He lacked probable cause to arrest the individual for suspicion of burglary, and in his zeal to arrest a burglary suspect, he becomes liable for tort action.

The intentional tort of assault and battery involves the case when a public officer who, under color of authority, without lawful necessity, assaults or beats an individual. Public officers, of course, have the authority to use reasonable force in effecting an arrest, preventing an escape, or overcoming resistance. However, if the force used by the public officer is designed to punish the arrestee and goes beyond the required force necessary to overcome resistance, to prevent escape, or to effect the arrest, the public officer is liable for an intentional tort. The following situation would be an example of an unlawful assault by a public officer. A drunk driver, driving recklessly at high speeds, leads public officers on a lengthy pursuit. Eventually the suspect is stopped, taken into custody for reckless and drunk driving and secured in the rear seat of a police vehicle. The suspect begins to shout obscenities at the officers, and an officer, whose nerves are unsettled from the high-speed pursuit, strikes the suspect in an attempt to cause him to stop the profane language. The force used against the suspect is in the form of punishment, even if prior force was required to take the suspect into custody.

Another intentional tort that affects public officers is wrongful death. Primarily, public officers may justifiably take a human life if they are attempting to overcome deadly resistance in effecting a legal process, if they are preventing the death of an innocent party, or if they are taking fleeing felons into custody. Two key words to consider in a justifiable death situation are "violence" and "felony." In cases where neither of these situations prevail, the public officer could be responsible for an intentional tort. Consider the following situation: A Caucasian, driving in a black section of town in the middle of the night, attracts the attention of two plainclothes black officers who, in an unmarked police car, attempt to pull up alongside of him to inform him that he is in the black part of town in a prostitution area. As the officers pull up beside the driver, they yell, "Police officers, pull over!" The driver becomes frightened, thinking they are dangerous because they are not in uniform and not in a black and white police car. After a high-speed pursuit, the officers pull the driver over to the curb. Instead of waiting for uniformed officers to arrive, they approach the car in an attempt to talk to the driver. The driver observes two large blacks not in uniform approaching him, and out of fear for his life he floors his vehicle and brushes one of the officers. The other officer shoots and kills the driver and has thereby committed an intentional killing. Although it may be a mistake, the officers could be liable for a wrongful death.

Unintentional torts (negligence) are a different matter. All people have the duty to act as reasonable, prudent persons or as required by law; Negligence comes about as follows: 1) if there has been a breach of that duty, 2) if the breach is the proximate and direct cause of an injury or damage, then a tort has been committed. There are hundreds of situations where torts can be alleged to have been committed. Consider the following examples. When a public officer functioning legitimately in an emergency situation accidently injures an innocent bystander, liability could result. For example, if a public officer is chasing a fleeing felon and in an attempt to halt the felon he fires a warning shot into the air, and if the warning shot injures an innocent bystander, then the public officer could be liable for negligence. There is also an obligation on the part of public officers to protect traffic accident scenes. If they do not position flares to route traffic around an existing traffic accident or position personnel for traffic direction, a collision and injury could result and they, along with their employer, could be liable for negligence. Public officers also have an obligation to protect incompetents, which include inebriated people, insane people, etc. For example, the town drunk is passed out in a bar and because he is not disturbing anyone the police officer allows him to stay inside the bar in a semi-conscious condition. Later, the drunk regains some of his stability and wanders out into the street and promptly gets run over by a vehicle. In this case, the officer could be liable for negligence due to the fact that he did not fulfill his obligation in protecting the incompetent. In the same barroom situation, liability could result if the drunk were to drive his car and become involved in an accident.

Historically, the legislatures declared that public employees and employers were immune from civil suit. Now, however, this governmental immunity has been stripped away by statuatory schemes allowing suit against public agencies, employers, and employees. However, public employees can only be sued for acts or omissions occurring within the course and scope of their employment in the manner allowed by governmental liability statutes. These statutes are intended to put the public employee, and the governmental entity which employs him, on notice of the claim so that prompt investigation may be undertaken. Usually, the statutes require that a written claim describing the acts or omissions of the public employees and the consequential damages be filed with the governmental entity employer on or before a particular date, such as the 100th day after the events complained of. The filing of this 100-day claim is a requirement that must be met before suit can be brought against public employees and employers.

Public employees sued for *negligent* acts or omissions occurring within the course and scope of their employment may be immune if they can prove that their conduct was discretionary rather than ministerial. Except as otherwise provided by statute, a public employee is not liable for an injury resulting from his act or omission where the act or omission was the result of the exercise of the discretion vested in him, whether or not such discretion was abused. This immunity extends to a law enforcement officer, exercising due care, in the execution or enforcement of any law. However, this immunity does not extend to liability for false imprisonment or false arrest.

It should be noted that public employees can be held liable for negligent performance of their ministerial duties, as distinguished from their discretionary acts. A discretionary act has been defined as one that requires personal deliberation, decision, and judgment, while a ministerial act amounts only to obedience to orders or performance of a duty to which an officer is left no choice of his own. Simply stated, a public employee may not be liable for failing to act, if the decision not to act is a discretionary one. But, if he decides upon a course of action, he could be liable for negligently or recklessly executing that course of action. Thus, a police officer may be immune from civil liability for the consequences of his decision not to arrest a person, although if he decides to arrest, he could be responsible for improper or careless execution of the arrest.

Similarly, an officer would not be liable if in his discretion he elected not to warn a potential victim of the release of a dangerous prisoner. However, if the officer promised to notify the potential victim and the victim felt he could rely on the officer's promise, the officer would be liable for the consequences of carelessly releasing the prisoner without warning the victim.

A public employee sued for negligent or careless acts or omissions occurring within the course and scope of public employment is entitled to indemnification by the public employer. However, intentional torts and grossly negligent or reckless conduct can result in judgment of punitive damages against the public employee. As punitive damages are intended to set an example and to punish the wrongdoer, public policy prohibits insurance for punitive damages. Similarly, public liability statutes exclude punitive damages levied against public employees from indemnification by public employers.

Claims against employees usually are brought against the employer as well. A claim for an intentional act (assault and battery) is usually based upon negligence as well. Employers and their insurance carriers are obligated to indemnify employees for acts of negligence but not for intentional acts resulting in punitive damages.

Since one incident can result in a judgment of both general damages based upon negligence and punitive damages based upon intent, an employee, whether public or private, is well-advised to demand in writing that the employer and insurance carrier settle the claim in order to prevent the employee from being exposed to punitive damages. Under certain jurisdictions, tendering a demand that the employer or carrier settle the claim will enable the employee to avoid the disruptive effects of a judgment for punitive damages, as refusal to settle may make the insurance carrier liable to the employee. The best advice for an employee facing a claim for punitive damages is to seek the counsel of an attorney not associated with either the employer or the employer's insurance carrier.

Endnotes

1. Joel Prentis Bishop, New Criminal Law 32 (Chicago: P. H. Flood, 8th ed. 1892).
2. Rollin M. Perkins, *Criminal Law and Procedures Cases and Materials* (New York: The Foundation Press, Inc., 1972).
3. People v. Beesley, 119 Cal App 82.
4. U.S. v. Harris, 347 U.S. 612.
5. Palmer v. The City of Euclid, Ohio, Supreme Court of the United States, 402, U.S. 544.

6. Coates v. The City of Cincinnati, 402, U.S. 611.
7. People v. Harris, 98 Cal App 2d 662.
8. James P. Turner, *The Civil Rights Act and Prosecution of Police Officers for Civil Rights Violations*, U.S. Department of Justice, Civil Rights Division, 1970.

QUESTIONS

1. Name five characteristics that must be present in order to validate a specific crime.
2. Give four definitions of crime and discuss how each differs.
3. List seven purposes of the criminal law.
4. What are the distinctions between crimes and torts?
5. Describe the relationship between the Fourteenth Amendment to the U.S. Constitution and civil and criminal liability concerning mistakes by law enforcement personnel.
6. Explain in detail the comprehensive scheme of tort legislation.
7. List the different intentional torts and unintentional torts and explain the difference.
8. Give examples of intentional tort and unintentional tort situations as they affect the criminal justice system.

Chapter Four

CLASSIFICATION AND APPLICATION OF CRIMES

THE FELONY, MISDEMEANOR, AND INFRACTION DISTINCTION

The common law recognized three major classes of crimes: treason, felony, and misdemeanor. Treason was the most serious because it was considered to be the most disruptive of social order. This class of offenses generally included plotting the overthrow of the crown, giving aid and comfort to enemies of the crown, counterfeiting the coin of the realm or the privy seal, and plotting to kill the chancellor or the king's justices. All of the above constituted high treason; one of the same acts against a lesser lord was petit (small) treason. In almost all cases, the penalty for treason was death and forfeiture of all property. The forfeiture penalty was especially significant for the medieval Englishman because it meant that all family lands and estates would return to the crown and that the offender's family and heirs would be deprived of the social status that land ownership conferred. This idea of "corruption of blood" (punishment for the offenses of the ancestor being visited upon the heirs) is so repugnant to the American jurisprudential philosophy that Article III, § 3 of the United States Constitution forbids it.

Under the common law, murder, manslaughter, rape, sodomy, robbery, larceny, arson, burglary and mayhem constituted the class of crimes designated as felonies. The penalty for these crimes was always forfeiture and additionally oftentimes death or other punishment of lesser severity, depending upon the seriousness of the offense and the culpability of the offender. Any crime defined by the crown not rising to the seriousness of treason or felony was a misdemeanor.

Most states recognize three classes of crimes, felonies, misdemeanors, and infractions. The felony-misdemeanor-infraction distinction is less clear in modern law than was the treason-felony-misdemeanor distinction at common law. As will be seen later, it is very important to determine the class of crime of which the defendant has been convicted or accused. This may be accomplished in various ways. First, the statute itself may specify the class of crime described. This is most common with infractions. Second, if the statute does not specifically classify the crime but does specify the punishment, then the crime is classified by the punishment spelled out in the statute. Third, if the statute specifies the punishment in the alternative (i.e., allows the judge to impose either misdemeanor or felony punishment), then the punishment actually imposed will determine whether the crime will be classified as a felony or misdemeanor. Most crimes are classified by the type of punishment provided for or the punishment actually imposed. The exception is in the case of infractions, which are generally classified as such by the statute proscribing certain behavior.

Generally, any crime that is punishable by imprisonment in the state prison is a felony, or any crime that is punishable by a term in the state prison or as an alternative by a term in the county jail is a felony if the actual sentence imposed is a term in state prison. Any crime that is punishable by a term in the county jail for no more than one year, or any crime that is punishable by a term in county jail or alternatively by a term in state prison is a misdemeanor if the sentence actually imposed is a term in county jail.

Infractions are generally petty offenses such as traffic violations. One accused of a felony or misdemeanor is constitutionally guaranteed the right to trial by jury and the right to appointed counsel in the case of indigency. The defendant accused of an infraction is entitled to neither a jury trial nor appointed counsel. An infraction, unlike the felony or misdemeanor, is never punished by a term in jail; the normal penalty is a small fine.

Quite apart from the immediate effects of the felony-misdemeanor-infraction distinction (such as the length of jail sentence or absence thereof), the future social, economic, and penal implications can be immense. Most professional and semi-professional licenses issued by the state will be revoked if the licensee is convicted of a felony or a misdemeanor involving moral turpitude whereas if the licensee were convicted of a simple misdemeanor, his license would often not be in jeopardy. Most states have criminal recidivism statutes that deal more harshly with each successive felony than with the first. These statutes add a number of years to the minimum sentence upon a second felony conviction; some statutes provide that upon three or more felony convictions, the convicted felon may be given a life term in prison.

These additional terms are quite independent of the sentence that the felon will receive for the actual commission of the second or third felony; they are separate from and added to such sentences. So under most such recidivism statutes, one convicted of a felony with two prior misdemeanors would only be punished for the felony involved, whereas one convicted of a felony with two prior felonies would be punished for the current felony and could receive a life sentence as well.

A convicted felon in most jurisdictions may suffer certain political disabilities that are not visited on one convicted of a misdemeanor. In some cases, the right to vote and to hold public office is restricted. Often one convicted of a felony may be impeached as a witness solely on the grounds that he is a convicted felon. This does not hold true of one convicted of a misdemeanor.

For the police officer, the distinction between a felony and a misdemeanor can be vital. Generally, an officer may only arrest for a misdemeanor committed in his presence and may not use deadly force to effect the arrest. But he may arrest for a felony upon the reasonable belief that such a felony has been committed in the recent past, though it may not have happened in his presence.

PUNISHMENT

Ask any ten people the question, "Should one who breaks the law be punished?" and chances are good that all ten would answer yes. Ask these same people, "Under what circumstances should one who breaks the law be punished?" and at least some would probably agree that perhaps there are circumstances under which one could break the law and be blameless. Ask these same ten people, "Why should one who breaks the law be punished?" and quite possibly no two would give the same reasons.

These three questions are among the most controversial philosophical questions in Western thought. They have been debated, argued, and answered by philosophers for centuries and still no society has reached a consensus. Perhaps before inquiring how the law answers these questions, it might be instructive to survey the various philosophical approaches to punishment.

To answer the first question affirmatively, one must agree that the wrongdoers could have acted differently than they did. Or put it another way, to be held morally and legally accountable for a wrongful act, the wrongdoer must have had a choice whether or not to act and chose to act in a manner that society finds blameworthy. Philosophers in the Western world generally have not had much of a problem with this question because of the belief in free will basic to Western Christian thought. So, let it be assumed that when one breaches the law, he ought to be punished.

Almost all philosophers, and indeed people in general, feel that under certain circumstances, one should be able to breach the law with impunity. Most would agree that one is justified in exceeding the speed limit to rush a seriously ill person to the hospital. The question then merely becomes, under what circumstances is one justified in breaking the law?

The third question of "Why punish?" is the

difficult one. All of the answers given to this question fall rather loosely into one or more of the following three categories.

Utilitarian Theories

Utilitarian theories hold that punishment is at best a necessary evil, justifiable if, and only if, the good of its consequences outweighs its own immediate and intrinsic evil. Punishment is pain or deprivation inflicted on a person for the sake of producing such a future good as correction or reform of the offender, protection of society against other offenses by the same offender, and especially deterrence of other would-be offenders through the threat of retribution.

The Retributive Theory

The theory of retribution holds that the primary justification of punishment is always to be found in the fact that an offense has been committed that deserves punishment, not because of any future advantage to be gained by its infliction for either society or the wrongdoer. He has done damage to society; society will do damage to him because he deserves it.

Vengeance Theories

Vengeance theories make much of the unhappy fact that when harmful wrongs are committed, there is among men a widespread and natural lust for vengeance. So these theorists tell us that if vengeance is not the Lord's, it should at least be the law's, but not man's. If we are to demand an eye for an eye, the law should exact the punishment in an orderly systematic manner. Nothing would be more socially disruptive than for each individual to avenge every real or imagined wrong done him.

Legal Aspects of Punishment

One notion that is very basic to Anglo-American law is that under certain circumstances, one who has done wrong should not be held accountable for his wrongdoing. Many examples of this can be seen in perusing a list of the statutory and common-law defenses to crimes. Insanity is always a defense to a crime on the theory that one who is insane is not responsible for his acts and hence blameless. Another example of this notion is that one who is forced to commit a crime will not therefore be punished. A third example may be seen in the treatment of juvenile offenders. It is possible for a very young offender to commit a felony and completely escape punishment. A variation to this theme is apparent in the degrees of murder. The law considers one who has killed in the "heat of passion" to be less blameworthy than one who does so after careful and rational consideration.

Another question that every legal system must answer is, "Should the punishment fit the crime or the moral culpability of the criminal?" In English common law, all felonies, no matter how serious, were punishable by death. Thus, we have accounts of a mere child of twelve years being hanged for stealing.

The man who stole bread to satisfy his hunger was punished as severely as the man, motivated by greed and avarice, who stole money. Fyodor Dostoevsky, the great Russian novelist, argues persuasively against this "punishment fit the crime" theory by pointing out that while two crimes may ostensibly appear to be the same, the moral culpability of the perpetrators may be quite unequal. Before any legal system can heed the admonition of Dostoevsky or emulate the early English, it must answer the question posed above, "Why punish?" If the state seeks retribution or vengeance, then it is justified in treating all thieves alike, but if it seeks to rehabilitate the thief or to deter his future criminal acts, then perhaps the state should inquire into the motives of the thief and punish him according to his moral culpability.

Probably most governments have no clearly defined reason for punishing a wrongdoer but rather seek to accomplish some or all of the following:

1. *To rehabilitate the wrongdoer.* To make him understand that he ought not commit a crime again because it is wrong and to teach him a useful occupation.
2. *To deter this wrongdoer* from future crime. Even if the wrongdoer is inclined to commit the crime again, the state will make the penalty so severe that he will forego future crime.
3. *To deter crime by others.* Use this wrongdoer as an example to other would-be wrongdoers.
4. *To keep this wrongdoer incarcerated* so that future crime on his part will be impossible.

5. *To avenge the wrongdoing* on the part of this wrongdoer.
6. *To uphold the majesty of the law.* Show this wrongdoer and others that when the law is broken, someone must pay.

The American legal system has generally agreed with Dostoevsky, hence our gradation of degrees of felonies, our elaborate provisions for probation for some convicted persons, and our habitual criminal statutes.

Two Supreme Court cases have announced the purpose of punishment.

> For some years, many courts and writers on criminal law and penology have held that the purpose of legally adjudicated punishment is not or should not be vengeance, but rather deterrence of the offender and other prospective offenders from crime, assistance in their rehabilitation, and the protection of society.

> Pain intentionally inflicted is relevant only to the extent that criminal penalties are designed to exact retribution for the evil done by criminals. Whatever may have been the fact historically, retribution is no longer considered the primary objective of the criminal law . . . and is thought by many not even to be a proper consideration . . . granted, however, that retribution may be a proper consid-

eration, it is doubtful that the penalty should be adjusted to the evil done without reference to the intent of the evildoer. Modern penology focuses on the criminal, not merely on the crime.[2]

Punishment of Crime

Most states have no clearly stated, coherent theory of punishment. The problem is that while all of the procedures and methods of punishment are clearly understood, it is not known what results are sought or desired. Some examples illustrate the problem.

Many criminal code sections exemplify this combination of theories of punishment under which our statutes are conceived. Portions of these sections provide that under certain circumstances, especially where the offender has no prior record and the offense committed is not serious, the probation department must furnish a report and recommend either probation or a jail term. Clearly, in this instance, the state has an eye toward the rehabilitation of the offender. For if the wrongdoer has committed an offense within the class of offenses for which probation may be granted, and the probation department deems that the likelihood of this offender committing a future offense is slight, the offender may completely escape incarceration. This is the "punishment to fit the offender" theory. Also, of the three philosophic theories of punishment aforementioned, this procedure is consistent with the utilitarian theory (i.e., that the rehabilitation of the offender is one of the legitimate aims of punishment).

Contrast this procedure with other criminal code

sections that prohibit the granting of probation for certain crimes. These crimes where probation is prohibited are deemed so serious or so disruptive of the social order that the perpetrator must be incarcerated. With which of the theories of punishment is this procedure consistent? Certainly it is not consistent with the rehabilitation of the criminal, for it is at least conceivable that the perpetrator of the most serious crime would profit more from controlled probation than from a term in state prison. Consider the theory that asserts that society punishes wrongdoers as an example to others. That theory would be consistent with the no probation provisions. The theory of vengeance (society punishes to prevent individuals from taking the punishment of criminals into their own hands) may also account for this procedure. However, the retributive theory (some acts by their very nature deserve punishment) probably best accounts for the no probation provisions discussed above.

If the above provisions are an accurate manifestation of the objectives of criminal punishment, it would appear that the states or at least the legislators therein are philosophic eclectics, for we seek at once to:

1. Rehabilitate
2. Hold up the convict as an example to other would-be wrongdoers
3. Exact vengeance and retribution

It is doubtful that any penal system can accomplish each and all of these, for some are, by their very nature, mutually exclusive. Practically, punishment is dispersed in two basic fashions, depending upon the state:

1. A convicted felon is placed under the control of a state agency that has the duty to decide how long the person will remain in the prison. This "indeterminate sentence" theory requires the state agency to abide by a minimum and a maximum penalty, for example, one to ten years or five years to life. The release date is not determined by the judge but rather by the state agency after the person has served part of his time.

   The justification and purpose of this theory is to allow flexibility for those who show marked and speedy rehabilitation. If the inmate shows that he has learned a trade, that he can adjust and control himself, and that he has improved in many other ways, then he should be released earlier than someone who has not improved himself at all.

   The criticism often levied against this system is that prisoners often have no "out date" in sight—confinement seems hopeless and endless. Also, some feel that the extent of punishment should be determined by judges rather than by a state bureaucracy.
2. The second basic method of determining punishment requires that the judge at the time of sentencing set a definite and certain term, for instance, three years in state prison, etc. The prison system itself is given some flexibility—such as reduced time for good behavior, for working, etc. The problem with this system, however, is that it

does not induce a person to work strenuously toward his own rehabilitation.

PRIOR CONVICTIONS AND INCREASED PENALTIES

Each state has a number of statutes that substantially increase the penalty for conviction of a crime if the offender has been previously convicted of certain specified crimes.[3] Some of these particular statutes will be discussed below, but first it might be instructive to inquire into the theoretical aspects of punishment for prior convictions. Taken together, the two cases cited above indicate that the purpose of punishment is not vengeance or retribution but rather is: 1) deterrence of the offender and other prospective offenders from crime, 2) assistance in the rehabilitation of criminals, and 3) the protection of society. Which of these objectives are accomplished by the statutes that punish repeat offenders more severely? They probably deter repeated offenses by the same person, but it is difficult to see how they would deter prospective offenders. They probably afford some degree of protection to society, but most likely they do not serve much rehabilitative function. So, in all likelihood, these statutes accomplish two legitimate aims of the penal system—protecting society and deterring the individual offender.

The Habitual Criminal Statute

[The habitual criminal statute] does not

> create a substantive offense, habitual criminality; rather it provides for more severe punishment, proportionate to their persistence in crime, of those who have proved immune to lesser punishment.[4]

> Prior convictions merely aggravate the position of one accused of the primary offense in that he is by reason of his former imprisonment placed in the classification of those who may never be reformed.[5]

Some statutes provide that one with two prior felony convictions is to be sentenced to life in prison. Sometimes a section will further specify that one with three prior convictions is to receive life imprisonment. These sections differ in that the period of eligibility for parole is different.

The offenses that bring these provisions into play are usually robbery; burglary of the first degree; burglary with explosives; rape with force or violence; arson; murder; assault with intent to commit murder; train wrecking; felonious assault with a deadly weapon; extortion; kidnaping; escape from a state prison by the use of force or dangerous or deadly weapons; rape, fornication, sodomy, or carnal abuse of a child under the age of fourteen years; or conspiracy to commit any one or more of the aforementioned felonies.

The prior felonies that make the statute operative, provided the offender stands currently convicted of one of the felonies enumerated above, are: robbery; burglary; burglary with explosives; rape with force or violence; arson; murder; assault with intent to commit murder; grand theft; bribery of a public official; perjury; subornation of perjury; train wrecking; feloniously receiving stolen goods; felonious assault with a deadly weapon; extortion; kidnaping; mayhem; escape from a state prison; rape, fornication, sodomy, or carnal abuse of a child under the age of fourteen years; or conspiracy to commit any one or more of the aforementioned felonies. The felonies to which the statute may be applied may have been committed in the home state or in any other state, but if committed in another state, the felony must be the equivalent of one of those enumerated in the statute.

If the state seeks to charge the defendant with habitual criminality and to punish him accordingly, it is necessary that the state allege the prior felonies and also charge in the accusatory pleading that the defendant served time in state prison. If the defendant denies the conviction of the prior felonies or of the service of time in state prison, the state must prove both at the trial. In its verdict, the jury must find that the defendant did in fact receive each of the alleged prior convictions and further, that the defendant served time in state prison for each of the prior convictions. The state must also allege and prove and the jury must find that each of the prior convictions was the result of a separate trial.

If the defendant so requires, the prosecution must also show that the prior conviction was obtained in a proper fashion; specifically, that the defendant's constitutional rights were upheld or knowingly waived. Once a defendant claims he did not understand what was happening during his old criminal proceedings, the prosecution must prove, if he entered a guilty plea, that he was fully advised of the following constitutional rights:

1. The right to a jury trial or court trial
2. The right to an attorney (court appointed, if the defendant is poor)
3. The right to confront and cross-examine witnesses against him
4. The right to remain silent and not incriminate himself by way of a guilty plea

Once advised, the prosecution must further show, by way of court records or transcripts, that the defendant knowingly and understandingly waived and gave up each enumerated right. There must not be the slightest hint of duress, pressure, or threats on the defendant. Only if all of the above rights of the defendant are proven to have not been violated can the prior conviction be used to increase punishment.

The other statutes that are closely related also deal with prior convictions. However, they are concerned with the use of firearms or deadly weapons. Many statutes provide that one who commits any felony while armed with a deadly weapon shall serve an additional amount of years in state prison. Upon the second, third and fourth convictions under like circumstances, the penalty may be increased even more often resulting in minimum terms of fifteen to twenty-five years and more. A few statutes reflect that the perpetrator need only be armed, while others require that he must *use* the firearm. These statutes often increase the penalties even more when the prior conviction involved an armed felony.

In summary, the following characteristics will often be used by a state legislature to increas penalties:

1. Prior felony conviction.
2. Prior convictions for certain enumerated crimes.
3. Prior *armed* felony conviction.
4. Multiple prior convictions.
5. Being armed at the time of commission of the present offense.
6. Being armed with a *concealed* deadly weapon *at the time of arrest.*
7. Using a weapon at the time of the present offense.
8. Inflicting injury on another during the commission of an offense.
9. Sometimes what would ordinarily be a misdemeanor is increased to a felony when there is a prior misdemeanor conviction for the same offense. (For example, a petty theft conviction followed by another petty theft will sometimes result in that second charge being classified and punished as a felony.)

MERGER AND INCLUDED OFFENSES

The doctrine by which certain crimes are said to be included in other larger or higher crimes is called *merger*, that is to say the lesser crime merges into the greater.

The Common-Law Rules

It is often the case that a single criminal act will result in the commission of multiple crimes, felonies or misdemeanors, or both. An example of this principle is illustrated by the two common-law crimes of robbery and larceny. Every robbery necessarily includes a larceny because the definition of a robbery is "a larceny by force." It is therefore impossible to commit a robbery without committing a larceny. Another example would be burglary and any other felony. The definition of a burglary is the breaking and entering of the dwelling house of another in the nighttime to commit a felony. The felony is not specified, and although it is normally larceny that is the object of the burglary, it also could be rape, murder, etc. A third example would be the common-law felony of mayhem, which is the disfigurement of another. It is impossible to commit this felony without also committing the misdemeanor, battery.

The common-law rule of merger was this: if a misdemeanor and a felony were committed in a single act, then the misdemeanor merged into the felony, and the offender, if tried on the felony, could not be convicted of the misdemeanor. The reason for this rule was that the procedures for trying the offender on misdemeanor charges and the procedures for trying him on felony charges often differed. However, if the offender committed two misdemeanors or two felonies by the same act, there was no merger.

In the first example given above, there would be no merger because each of the crimes committed is a felony. This is also true of example two. However, there would be a merger in example three because the crime of mayhem is a felony, and the crime of battery is a misdemeanor, so the battery charge would merge into the mayhem charge.

The above rules do not apply unless both crimes are accomplished by the same act or transaction. This is a question of fact to be determined in a court of law. The court must determine whether the defendant committed one or multiple acts and if multiple acts were committed, were they so related so as to constitute a single transaction.

Merger of Conspiracy

In the common law, conspiracies were misdemeanors so by the rules above, if the object of the conspiracy was a felony and the felony was completed, the conspiracy merged into the completed act. This was not the case if the object of the conspiracy was a misdemeanor. Whether or not the misdemeanor was complete was of no import, because a misdemeanor did not merge into a misdemeanor and the conspirator-misdemeanant could be prosecuted for both.

Merger of Attempts

The rules for the merger of an attempted crime into the crime itself were identical to the rule of merger of conspiracies cited above. Any attempted crime at common law was a misdemeanor; thus, if the completed crime was a felony, then the attempt merged into the completed crime. However, if the completed crime was a misdemeanor, then there could be no merger, and the misdemeanant could be convicted of both the crime and the attempt.

Included Offenses—The Modern Law

The concept of merger has somewhat less viability in modern law than it had at common law. The rules cited above regarding the merger of felonies and misdemeanors do not realistically apply today. A closely related doctrine in modern law, however, is that of included offenses. Technically speaking, merger and included offenses are part of the same doctrine. If an offense is lesser and necessarily included, it is said to merge into the greater offense, and the offender has legally committed only the greater offense. Like the common law doctrine of merger, the modern law doctrine of included offenses has no application unless the offender has committed multiple crimes with a single act. When the defendant is convicted or acquitted or has been once placed in jeopardy upon an accusatory pleading, the conviction, acquittal, or jeopardy is a bar to another prosecution for the offense charged in such accusatory pleading, for an attempt to commit the same, or for an offense *necessarily included* therein of which he might have been convicted under that accusatory pleading. Stated simply with respect to included offenses, this precludes dual prosecution where the defendant has committed two crimes with a single act and where the one act is necessarily included within the other. It only remains to determine what constitutes a necessarily included offense.

> The test of a necessarily included offense is simply that where an offense cannot be committed without necessarily committing another offense, the latter is a necessarily included offense.[6]

> It is clear that where an offense cannot be accomplished without necessarily committing another offense, the latter is a necessarily included offense. If, in the commission of acts denounced by one statute, the offender must always violate another, the one offense is necessarily included in the other.[7]

> Thus, a strict test has been developed, based on the elements of the crime as defined in the particular criminal statute: A crime is an included offense if all of its elements are also elements of the other crime, so that substantially the same facts would be required to prove the commission of either. And a crime is not an included offense if any of its elements is not an element of the other crime, so that one requires proof of some fact in addition to the facts required to establish the other.[8]

And this doctrine is applied in reverse also.

> Where prosecution for the included offense is first, and there is an *acquittal*, the defendant may not thereafter be tried for the greater, for if he is not guilty of the lesser included offense he cannot be guilty of the greater. A conviction of the lesser is held to be a bar to prosecution for the greater on the theory that to convict of the greater would be to convict twice of the lesser.[9]

So it can be seen that it is not so much a case of two crimes merging and becoming one, but a case of the prosecution choosing which crime to prosecute, the greater or the lesser. And once the defendant has been tried on either, the prosecution is barred from prosecuting on the other. This case is actually more an example of the doctrines of bar and double jeopardy, developed more fully in the next section.

Merger of Conspiracies at Modern Law

Supreme Court Justice William O. Douglas, speaking for the majority of the Court in *Pinkerton* v. *United States*, 328 U.S. 640 (1946), states very clearly the law in the United States on the merger of conspiracies into the completed crime:

> The common-law rule that the substantive offense, if a felony, was merged in the conspiracy, has little vitality in this

> country. It has been long and consistently recognized by the Court that the commission of the substantive offense and a conspiracy to commit it are separate and distinct offenses. . . . A conviction for the conspiracy may be had though the substantive offense was completed. . . . And the plea of double jeopardy is no defense to a *conviction for both offenses*. . . . It is only an identity of offenses which is total. . . . A partnership in crime . . . It has ingredients, as well as implications, distinct from the completion of the unlawful object.

In modern times, there is no merger of the conspiracy and the completed crime. A conspiracy is not included in the completed crime, and a conviction of the completed crime is no bar to conviction on the conspiracy.

Merger of Attempts at Modern Law

If the defendant has been convicted on the completed crime, thus placed in jeopardy, then that jeopardy would preclude his being tried for the attempt. Again, this is more akin to the doctrines of bar and double jeopardy than that of merger.

Summary

At common law, the doctrine tended to be an outgrowth of the rules of criminal procedure. In modern times, the doctrine of included offenses is more a due process concept. Modern courts consider it fundamentally unfair to convict a person for multiple crimes when the commission of one crime is necessary to the commission of the other. However, the doctrines of included offenses and merger both require that the single act or transaction test be passed. But that is not to say that if the crimes derive from the same act or transaction, they may not both be prosecuted. That was not the common-law rule, nor is it the law today. Recall, at common law, a felony did not merge into a felony, or a misdemeanor did not merge into a misdemeanor even though they both derived from the same act. In modern law, one may fire a single shot, kill two people, and be tried for two murders. One crime is not necessarily included in the other.

CAPITAL CRIMES

The death penalty was constitutional prior to 1972. Most states provided for the death penalty for violation of the following types of crimes: 1) murder, 2) treason, 3) kidnapping with bodily harm, 4) perjury that leads to the death of an innocent person, 5) assault by a life convict on a prison guard, or 6) conspiracy to commit any of the above-mentioned crimes.

The California Supreme Court was one of the first state courts to deem the death penalty unconstitutional. They did so on February 18, 1972. Earlier, the California Supreme Court had repeatedly held the death penalty to be legally sound and a question for the legislature to decide. The death penalty procedure before February 18, 1972, was that in most cases, the defendant, if found guilty of a capital offense, would be given a trial in which the judge or jury would determine the penalty and whether or not the defendant would be executed. This system of a separate penalty phase to determine punishment was upheld by the U.S. Supreme Court just prior to the California decision.

In *People* v. *Anderson,* the whole process was struck down.[10] The state court held that the death penalty was unconstitutional under the state constitution and did not rule on its constitutionality under the federal Bill of Rights. The state supreme court held that since the state constitution read, "cruel or unusual punishment," and the federal Constitution read, "cruel and unusual punishment," the death penalty could be discarded on state grounds because of the "or," meaning that the death penalty could be found invalid if it were either cruel or unusual. The *Anderson* decision was written in such a way that arguably, it could not be interfered with by the U.S. Supreme Court; specifically because the state court held the death penalty unconstitutional under purely state grounds. The U.S. Supreme Court can only decide cases under federal statutes and the federal Constitution and may not interfere with state constitutions unless they are in conflict with federal law. The state supreme court ruled that under evolving standards of decency, the death penalty became both "cruel and unusual," and therefore, it had to be judicially abolished under the state constitution. The effect of the *Anderson* decision was to free every person on death row from a sentence of death and to hold the death penalty unconstitutional in California until the new statutes reinterpreting the death penalty in a proper way were to take effect. Whether or not the new statutes will be upheld remains to be seen.

On June 29, 1972, the U.S. Supreme Court decided the cases of *Furman* v. *Georgia, Jackson* v. *Georgia,* and *Branch* v. *Texas,*[11] handing down a diversity of opinions regarding the status of the death penalty. Five justices agreed that the death penalty was unconstitutional in regard to the three above-mentioned defendants before the court. The four remaining justices had dissenting opinions.

However, it is important to note that the U.S. Supreme Court in effect held the death penalty unconstitutional *only* in regard to these cases. Only two of the justices held that the death penalty is unconstitutional in all cases; one justice, on the other hand, ruled that the death penalty would be constitutional under narrowly drawn statutes punishing especially heinous crimes that would carry a mandatory death penalty.

In total, the decision appears to mean that a majority of the justices would rule the death penalty to be constitutional if: 1) it was made mandatory (or perhaps allowing limited discretion in certain cases) in carefully drafted statutes as punishment for especially heinous crimes, or 2) it could be shown the death penalty would not be applied in a discriminatory manner. It appears that the U.S. Supreme Court differs from the state supreme court. The U.S. Supreme Court may ask the legislature to re-evaluate the necessity and need of capital punishment and if the legislature feels the need is present, to readopt legislation so that the death penalty would be narrowly drawn and could in no way be applied in a discriminatory fashion. Thus, no state supreme court has abolished the death penalty. They have merely asked that it be looked at with fresh eyes and be applied in an impartial manner.

The biggest complaint the justices of the U.S. Supreme Court had of the death penalty was its apparent lack of impartiality and its haphazard use. Too often in many of the southern states, the death penalty was used as a tool in racial discrimination—for example, two of the defendants in the U.S. Supreme Court cases were black men who had been convicted of the rape of white women. The court felt that whether or not one received the death penalty was often a matter of chance and luck, depending on the jury one drew and the biases of the triers of fact.

It appears that if death penalty crimes can be made more specific by state legislatures (for example, any premeditated murder; slaying of law enforcement personnel and prison guards; killing that results from skyjacking, kidnapping, or bombing; and murder torture of children), the U.S. Supreme Court would be prone to uphold a death penalty case. Many states have enacted legislation to reinstate the death penalty[12] since the decision by the Supreme Court deeming it unconstitutional. The state of New York legislated a new death penalty law, but in June of 1973, the New York State Supreme Court ruled that the state's death penalty for killing a policeman was unconstitutional. The court held that the law allowed too much discretion to juries to pass the test laid down by the U.S. Supreme Court. New York's statutes allowed juries, by unanimous vote, to set execution as the penalty for murderers of on-duty policemen or prison guards, or for murder committed by someone already under a life sentence. The New York Supreme Court held that the U.S. Supreme Court's ruling on the death penalty required strict standards in any death penalty statute to insure that the penalty would be imposed without discrimination.[13]

In October 1975, the Illinois Supreme Court declared that state's death penalty unconstitutional. The Illinois death penalty was instituted in 1973 and it contained essentially the same elements as the New York death penalty. The last year in which an execution was carried out in Illinois was 1964.

Endnotes

1. People v. Friend (1957) 47 C2d 749.
2. People v. Love (1960) 53 C.2d 843.
3. For example, see: California Penal Code sections 644, 12022, 3024, and 666.
4. *In re* McVickers (1946) 29 C.2d 264).
5. People v. Dunlop (1951) 102 C.A. 2d 314.
6. People v. Greer (1947) 30 C2d 589.
7. People v. Krupa (1944) 64 C.A.2d 592.
8. Bernard Ernest Witkin, *California Crimes*, I (San Francisco: Bender-Moss, 1963), p. 200.
9. Supra, note 7.
10. People v. Anderson 6 Cal 3d 628.
11. Furman v. Georgia (1973) 408 U.S. 238 Jackson v. Georgia (1972) 408 U.S. 238 Branch v. Texas (1972) 408 U.S. 238.
12. In September of 1973, the California legislature reenacted the death penalty making the punishment mandatory for persons convicted of the

following 11 crimes: (1) murder of an on-duty police officer or prison guard; (2) multiple slayings; (3) murder for hire; (4) murder to prevent a witness to a crime from testifying; (5) murder by a person who has a prior first degree murder conviction; and murder connected robbery, kidnapping, rape, burglary, child molesting, and trainwrecking resulting in death.

13. State of New York v. Fitzpatrick.

QUESTIONS

1. Identify and differentiate the three classifications of crime.
2. Review the reasons given in the chapter for governments punishing wrongdoers and draw personal conclusions about each reason.
3. List the statutes that serve to substantially increase the penalty for conviction of a crime if the offender has been previously convicted of certain specified crimes.
4. Identify the common-law and modern-law rules that serve to explain merger or lesser and included offenses.
5. What effect did the *Furman*, *Jackson*, and *Branch* cases have upon the death penalty in the United States?
6. Describe the factors necessary in a new death penalty statute to guarantee that it would not be declared unconstitutional.

Chapter Five

ELEMENTS OF CRIME

It is a time-honored proposition that the existence of a crime requires two essential elements. One is external, consisting of an act or omission prohibited by the criminal law. The other is internal and is generally referred to as criminal intent, guilty knowledge or intent, or *mens rea.*[1] Before any criminal sanctions can be imposed upon one's behavior, there must exist these indispensable elements.

INTENT

Common law dictated the principle that a crime is not consummated if the mind of the person doing the prohibited act is innocent. Every true crime (which are those other than regulatory or public welfare offenses) requires the presence of a criminal intent, or *mens rea.*

Much difficulty arises when an accurate and useful definition of *mens rea* is sought. Simply speaking, *mens rea,* or criminal intent, is a mental state of mind that is required to lead to criminal liability for a particular crime.

Criminal intent has been stated as nothing more than the intentional doing of that which the law declares to be a crime.[2] Intent to violate the law or to do a wrong is not a necessary element or condition for criminal intent. Thus, criminal intent exists whenever a person intentionally does that which the law declares to be a crime, even though he may not know that he is in fact committing a crime or that his act is wrong. (Ignorance of the law is no excuse—a simplistic but necessary rule.)

Lack of actual knowledge regarding the legal impropriety of an act is generally never a defense to a criminal offense and hence has no effect or has no real role in the composition of the *mens rea* element. This result is predicated upon the principle that knowledge of the law is imputed to everyone and consequently need not be demonstrated in a criminal prosecution.[3]

The term *mens rea*, or criminal intent, actually encompasses a number of different mental states. For some situations, a type of negligence can supply the criminal intent without the necessity of an "intentional" act. In other situations, the *mens rea* element of a crime may require more than general criminal intent, or an intentional act. In such circumstances, a specific intent to do a specific prohibited act may be necessary for conviction.

Criminal Negligence

Negligence in civil law has been defined as conduct that falls below the standard established by law for the protection of others against unreasonable risk of harm.[4] It can be characterized as a deviation from a standard of due care that causes or subjects others to foreseeable risks of harm. Mere negligence or carelessness of the kind discussed in civil actions and in tort law is not sufficient to establish criminal liability. Something more is needed before the conduct is of such character as to be worthy of criminal punishment.

It is generally held that the negligence of the accused must be "culpable," "gross," or "reckless," that is, the conduct of the accused must be such a departure from what would be the conduct of an ordinarily prudent or careful person under the same circumstances as to be incompatible with a proper regard for human life, or the conduct of the accused must amount to an indifference to consequences.[5] Such indifference to foreseeable or probable consequences is said to take the place of criminal intent. In a situation where the actor is recklessly disregardful of the foreseeable consequences of his acts, he is presumed to intend the natural consequences thereof.

Situations which involve criminal negligence are mostly encountered in homicide or manslaughter cases. It has been held that one who drives a car with knowledge of the fact that he may at any time have an attack of vertigo during which he will be unable to control a moving car and who has been cautioned not to drive alone, is guilty of manslaughter if such driving causes a fatal accident and is guilty of assault and battery if a nonfatal injury results.[6] An automobile is an extremely dangerous instrument, and if there exists a distinct possibility that the driver may cause the car to go out of control at any time, it raises such an obvious risk to human life that operation of the car would constitute reckless and wanton misconduct. If injury results, the driver must assume the criminal responsibility.

Other examples of gross negligence that would constitute a criminal act would be:

1. A person, without any intention of harming anyone, playfully fires a gun over the heads of his friends who are approaching his house. A neighbor is accidentally killed by the bullet. Manslaughter or possibly even murder charges would be the result because of his grossly negligent act.
2. A person under the influence of alcohol competes in a drag race with another vehicle; a bystander is killed in the ensuing accident. Such a reckless and grossly negligent act would constitute manslaughter in most jurisdictions.

Specific Intent

A general criminal intent is sufficient in all cases in which a specific intent or mental state is not required by the law defining the crime. Unless a criminal statute expressly requires a specific intent, a general intent is sufficient.[7]

Some offenses call for something more than a general *mens rea,* or blameworthy state of mind. Common illustrations of such crimes include any attempt of: assault with intent to commit felony, assault with caustic chemicals, administering poison with intent to kill, kidnapping for extortion, child stealing, larceny, robbery, burglary, issuing a check to defraud, and forgery.[8] Any additional mental requirement over and above an intent to commit the deed that constitutes the crime may be spoken of as a special mental element, or *mens rea.*[9]

Larceny serves as a good example of a crime that requires something more than the intent to do the act that constitutes the crime of larceny. Larceny in common law, is defined as the trespassory taking and carrying away of personal property of another with the intent to steal. The intent to steal can be characterized as an intent to permanently misappropriate. Thus, the "intentional" taking of property owned by another is not larceny if the actor intended to return such property at a later date. The act of taking may be intentional and trespassory, but if the intent to steal or permanently deprive is lacking, the common-law crime of larceny is not consummated. The specific intent necessary to establish larceny is therefore the mental state of mind to steal or permanently deprive the owner of his goods.

A related, but yet completely separate theory is the requirement of malice that is specified in some crimes. Malice can be simply defined as an intentional act done with ill will. However, malice or malicious behavior as found in the definition of a crime does not necessarily have the popular meaning of ill will, hatred, or anger toward the victim of the crime. It is true that in the offense of malicious mischief, it is generally held that the offender must have a feeling of personal revenge toward the property or toward the owner of the property involved, but in other crimes it usually means that the act was done willfully, intentionally, and without any legal justification or excuse. Perkins defines malice as an intent to do either the harm done or harm of a similar nature, or as the wanton and willful disregard of an obvious likelihood of causing such harm. This definition carries an implied negation of any justification, excuse, or mitigation for the act.[10]

Malice aforethought, a state of mind required by common-law murder, is a technical term. Although its earlier definitions described it as meaning a wicked, depraved, and malignant spirit, today it is generally said to mean a knowledge of such circumstances that according to common experience, there is a plain and strong likelihood that death will follow the contemplated act. Malice aforethought also implies a negation of any excuse or justification for said act. Basically, in the crime of murder, malice can be defined as "a man-endangering state of mind." There are many man-endangering states of mind, and they can be defined as follows: 1) a deliberate intention to take a human life; 2) a deliberate intention to cause great bodily harm; 3) doing an act without regard for the consequences, thus causing death in an unlawful manner; 4) death, unintentional or intentional, that occurs during the commission of felonies; and 5) death that occurs while resisting arrest.

Transferred Intent

The idea of transferred intent first appeared in a criminal case;[11] however, the doctrine has had more extensive and enthusiastic application in tort or civil-law cases. If the defendant shoots or strikes at A, intending to wound or kill him, and unforeseeably hits B instead, he is liable to B for an intentional tort.[12] The intent to commit a battery upon A is connected to the resulting injury to B; it is "transferred" from A to B.[13]

The tort concept of transferred intent has often been repudiated by courts in criminal prosecutions, and it is generally felt that the doctrine has no proper place in criminal law. The doctrine can be simply stated that when a man meaning one wrong does another that he does not mean to do, he is still punishable unless some specific intent is required. The reason sometimes offered is that the thing done, having proceeded from a corrupt mind, is to be viewed the same whether the corruption was of one particular form or another.[14]

This doctrine is strictly construed by the criminal courts and is only allowed to operate where a similar mental pattern exists between the intended act and the act actually committed. Where the state of mind that prompted the action does not constitute the particular *mens rea* required by law for the offense charged, the courts have not hesitated to repudiate the notion of transferred intent.[15] In the *Faulkner* case,[16] the defendant went into the hold of a ship to steal some rum. He then bored a hole in a cask and held a lighted match in his hand to see where to put a spike in the hole out of which the rum was running. The rum caught fire, and the ship was destroyed. The defendant was tried and convicted of maliciously setting fire to a ship on the high seas. The reviewing court quashed the conviction because the case was submitted to the jury on the transferred-intent theory. The intent to steal is not the same intent or mental state necessary to constitute the crime of maliciously setting fire to the ship. In another case, it was held that the killing of a horse by a shot fired with the intent of killing a person is not sufficient of itself to support a conviction of maliciously killing a horse.[17] However, where a party starts a fire for the purpose of maliciously burning A's house, and instead B's house is destroyed, the party is guilty of arson. The same mental element is present in the intended act and the resulting act. The actor maliciously intended to burn A's house—the requisite mental state necessary to establish arson with regard to B's house.

ACT

An act is basically an occurrence which results from an exertion of the will manifested in some overt form. An act, therefore, connotes a volitional movement. Occurrences that take place wholly independently of the will are not acts that constitute criminal offenses. A muscle spasm which causes a trigger to be pulled on a gun thereby discharging the weapon and causing death is not an act which establishes murder.

Several reasons have been given in justification for the requirement of an act. One is that a person's thoughts are not susceptible to proof, except when demonstrated by outward actions. Most persuasive, however, is the notion that the criminal law should not be so broadly defined so as to reach those who entertain criminal schemes in mind only but never let their thoughts govern their conduct.[18]

The act necessary for a crime varies with each particular crime and is defined generally by statute. Acts which ultimately culminate in criminal liability are broad and take many forms. An act can take the form of either active or passive participation or of an omission to act where there is a legal duty to do so. Hence, an act can be characterized as positive or negative, an act of commission or omission, the latter referring to leaving undone something that ought to be done.

For criminal liability to be based upon a failure or omission to act, there must be a legal duty and not just a moral duty to act. A moral duty to take affirmative steps is insufficient to create a legal duty to act. If a bystander witnesses a child being struck by a car, there is no legal duty to render aid or procure medical help. Most people would certainly recognize a moral compulsion to act under such circumstances, however, apathetic indifference in such a situation is not a crime punishable by law. Legal duty to act can be created by statutory imposition such as with the duty to pay taxes, the duty to pay child support, and the duty to stop and render aid to injured victims when such injury was accidentally inflicted by the party while operating an automobile.[19]

A duty may also arise in some instances irrespective of any statutory source. A duty could arise out of contract or possibly out of the relationship of the parties. Where one contracts to care for an elderly, sickly woman, a legal duty arises to render care, and a negligent omission could be manslaughter.[20] It is widely recognized that if a "good Samaritan" embarks upon a course of conduct to render aid to an accident victim, a duty arises for him to use reasonable care in his endeavors. A reckless mishandling may result in a manslaughter conviction.

CONCURRENCE OF ACT AND INTENT

Assuming that the *mens rea* and the act of a crime are established, before a criminal conviction can be sustained, it must be shown that the two elements have concurred. There must be a concurrence of the thought or intent coupled with the requisite act necessary to constitute the crime. In every crime or public offense, there must exist a union or joint operation between the act and the intent or criminal negligence. If A forms the intent to murder B but is subsequently forced to kill B out of self-defense, A is not chargeable with murder. The intent to murder did not coincide or concur with the act of killing. A most dramatic illustration is found in a case where the defendant attempted to kill a girl in Ohio. Thinking that he was successful, he took her body to Kentucky and cut off her head to prevent identification of the corpse, firmly convinced that she was dead at the time. He was in fact mistaken, and the act of decapitation was the cause of death. The defendant was convicted of murder, his defense being that there was in actuality no concurrence of act and intent because there was no intent to kill when the body was decapitated as he thought she was already dead. Fortunately, the conviction was upheld on the grounds that the defendant had set out to murder the girl and had caused her death in the perpetration of his plan.[21] The court determined that the whole scheme or plan was tainted with murderous intent and that there was ultimately a concurrence of intent and the act of killing.

CAUSATION

Where injury, death, or some form of harm constitutes the criminal offense, there must exist a causal relationship between the defendant's act and the resulting harm. Without such a causal connection, the defendant would not be criminally responsible for the offense. The causal relation is said to be present where the defendant's act or omission to act was the actual and proximate cause of the prohibited harm. Actual cause is satisfied where the defendant's conduct by itself or in combination with other factors has contributed in more than a trivial degree in bringing about the prohibited harm. It is not necessary that the defendant's conduct be the single or sole contributing factor. If A and B, acting independently, shot C, and C's death resulted from a loss of blood from both wounds, each act of shooting could be considered the actual cause, thus both actors would be chargeable with homicide.

Often, a "but for" test is applied to determine culpability. According to the "but for" test, the defendant's conduct must be an essential ingredient in producing the harm. "But for" the defendant's conduct, would the injury or harm have occurred at this time and in this manner? If a negative response is in order, the conduct is deemed an essential contributing factor and therefore an actual cause. Where A shoots B in the abdomen, thereby inflicting a mortal wound, A is criminally liable if B cuts his own throat on his death bed, producing immediate death.[22] Applying the "but for" test, the question arises as to whether the death of B would have occurred at this time and in this manner "but for" the original act of shooting? The original shooting inflicted an ultimately mortal wound; recognizing this fact, B cut his throat to hasten death. If A had refrained from shooting B, the death would not have occurred in this manner and at this time. Hence, the actual cause is established.

In some situations, the substantial factor test is applied in lieu of the "but for" test. Where A mortally wounds X and acting independently, B also inflicts a mortal wound on X, the "but for" test is not applicable to the individual acts. X would have died regardless of the wound inflicted by B. However, each wound can be considered a substantial factor in producing death where both wounds combine and the ultimate result is death. Each wound is therefore considered the actual cause, and both actors are criminally responsible for the homicide.

Actual cause is also the proximate cause where there exists no intervening acts or forces to break the chain of causation. Proximate cause is generally referred to as that cause that, in natural and continuous sequence unbroken by an efficient intervening cause, produces the chain of events without which the result would not have occurred.

An intervening cause is one that is neither operating in the defendant's presence, nor at the place where the defendant's act takes effect, nor at the time of defendant's act, but that comes into operation at or before the time of the damage.[23] If a strong wind is blowing at the time of an act, and the act produces a harmful result, the wind is not an intervening cause. This is considered a set stage. However, if the wind suddenly blows after the defendant's act and prior to injury, such an occurrence is considered an intervening act or force. For example, if A throws a rock at a target and a sudden gust of wind hurls the projectile in another direction causing it to strike B, the sudden gust is deemed an intervening act or force. To determine whether or not an intervening act or force is sufficient to break the chain of causation in the sense that the defendant's conduct will not be considered the proximate cause, it must be ascertained whether or not the intervening force is dependent or independent.

An independent intervening act is one that operates upon the situation created by the defendant and not in response thereto or as a result thereof. It can be generally classified as an act of God or an occurrence beyond the control of the defendant that came into operation regardless of his conduct. It may even be an act of another person or animal that would have taken place notwithstanding any act of the defendant. An intervening independent act is considered sufficient to break the chain of causation or supersede the defendant's conduct. Suppose A struck B and rendered him unconscious under a freeway overpass. Several minutes later an earthquake caused the collapse of the structure thereby crushing B's unconscious body. Applying the "but for" test, actual cause may be established. But for A rendering B unconscious, he would not have been present under the structure during the earthquake and hence would not have been killed. However, the earthquake is attributable to an act of God and thus is considered an independent act that severs the causal connection. No proximate cause exists between A's act and the death of B. In a more common example, if a drunk drives his vehicle into a highway work crew, killing one of the crew, a jury would be required to determine whether or not the failure to have proper warning signs and barriers erected was the proximate cause of the accident as opposed to the drunken driver. Does the work crew's omission constitute an independent intervening cause?

It is usually conceded that if an independent act is reasonably foreseeable, it will not be allowed to supersede the act of the defendant. Where A handcuffs B to a railroad track, and B is subsequently run over by a train, A will be held criminally liable. The occurrence of the train upon the scene is an independent act or event; however, the foreseeability factor precludes it from breaking the causal relation.

A dependent cause is one that operates as a result of or in response to the situation created by the defendant's conduct. It is a response or reaction to the defendant. A dependent intervening act does not break the causal chain unless it is clearly an abnormal response. It is the policy of the law to hold a defendant responsible for results caused by a dependent intervening act unless the particular act is highly unusual and unforeseeable. In a case where a man shot at some boys in a boat, merely intending to scare them, and one of the boys jumped into the water and was drowned, a conviction of manslaughter was upheld.[24] The decedent's act of jumping into the water was in response to the shooting and could be considered a normal reaction in that he was seeking safety. The responsive or dependent act will not therefore break the causal chain, and the defendant will be held responsible.

Medical treatment of a victim is most illustrative of this situation. If injury is inflicted and if death actually occurs as a result of medical treatment, the party who inflicted the original injury may be held criminally liable for the resulting homicide. Medical treatment is considered a dependent act since it is in response to the situation created by the defendant. Grossly negligent or erroneous medical treatment, on the other hand, is classified as an abnormal response and thus supersedes the original misconduct.[25]

CORPUS DELICTI

The term *corpus delicti* means "the body of the crime" or, in other words, the essential distinguishable elements of a criminal offense. *Corpus delicti* plays an important role in criminal procedure. To sustain the burden of proof in a criminal case, the prosecution must first establish that a crime has been committed. This is done where the *corpus delicti* has been proven by competent evidence. Failure by the prosecution to show the *corpus delicti* is a basic defense to a criminal charge.

Corpus delicti consists of two elements, facts establishing injury, loss, or harm and the criminal agency causing them to exist.[26] The prosecution need only prove the existence or commission of a crime to satisfy the *corpus delicti* requirement. The prosecution need not link or identify the accused as the perpetrator of the crime. The identity of the participants in a crime is not a necessary element of the *corpus delicti.*[27] Obviously, if a conviction is to be sustained, the prosecution must later establish beyond a reasonable doubt that the accused was the perpetrator. This burden of proof has no relation to establishing the body of the offense or the *corpus delicti.* The concept of *corpus delicti* in criminal law is principally used in connection with reducing the possibility of punishing a person for a crime that was never in fact committed.[28]

The corpus delicti rule that is universally followed dictates that no criminal conviction can be based upon a defendant's extrajudicial confession or admission, although otherwise admissible, unless there is other evidence tending to establish the *corpus delicti.*[29] Thus, even though a suspect has made a tape-recorded confession to a burglary, he can not be convicted if the owner of the house has died because no one can establish that the house was entered without permission and that property was stolen. To authorize a conviction, the *corpus delicti* must be established beyond a reasonable doubt; but in order to introduce a confession, the prosecution need only prove by slight evidence that a crime has been committed.

Many *corpus delicti* cases are homicide cases, where the difficulty may be that the victim simply disappeared and no dead body can be produced, or that, although a dead body is found, examination of the body and the surrounding circumstances reveals that the death may have been caused by accident, suicide, or natural causes as opposed to foul play.[30] In such cases, the defendant's extrajudicial confession is inadmissible to establish the *corpus delicti.* There must be independent evidence to corroborate such a confession before it is admissible in a court of law. The independent evidence need only tend to show that the deceased died, not as a result of natural or accidental causes, but by some criminal agency. "Tending to show" is interpreted to mean more likely than not; evidence of an independent nature is insufficient if it points no more in one direction than in the other. If a body is found, and there exists an even probability that death was attributable to natural causes rather than to some criminal agency, there is insufficient evidence to corroborate any extrajudicial confessions and such admission is prohibited.

ATTEMPTS

An attempt to commit a crime has been a common-law offense since the early 1800s. Attempts were misdemeanors in the common law regardless of whether the attempted crime was classified as a felony or a misdemeanor.

What constitutes an attempt is not always clear-cut, and no general rule will serve as a test in all cases. An attempt has been defined as an overt act done with the intent to commit a crime, and that, except for the interference of some cause preventing the carrying out of the intent, would have resulted in the commission of the crime. A typical statutory definition of attempt is as follows: every person who attempts to commit any crime but fails, or is prevented or intercepted in the perpetration thereof, is guilty of an attempt to commit a crime. In committing an attempt, the offender takes steps in the furtherance of an offense that he intends to carry out if he can.

The crime of attempt has two elements: 1) a specific intent to commit a particular offense, and 2) a direct ineffectual overt act toward its commission. The essence of the crime lies in the intention rather than in the acts done in furthering it. But, of course, the prosecution must establish not only the fact that the steps taken by the accused were inspired by the intention to go on to reach a desired objective constituting a specific crime, but also that the step was in point of law one that marked the commencement of the offense. Mere intention to commit a crime is not punishable, and an attempt occurs when the perpetrator commits an overt act in the furtherance of his intent toward the completion of the crime intended. Mere agreement by two or more people is not enough to complete the crime of an attempt; there must be an overt act accompanying the agreement, and this act must go beyond an act of preparation. According to many authorities, mere acts of preparation not proximately leading to the consummation of the intended crime (for example, obtaining tools or weapons) will not suffice to establish an attempt to commit it, especially when made at a distance from the place where the intended offense is to be committed. There must be some act moving directly toward the commission of the offense after the preparations are made. In order to establish an attempt, it must appear that the defendant had a specific intent to commit a crime and did a direct unequivocal act toward that end; preparation alone is not enough—some appreciable fragments of the crime must have been accomplished.[31]

The following cases are examples of attempts. A suspect enters a business armed with a weapon with the intent to commit a robbery then leaves because of crowded conditions.[32] However, the crime would not have been complete when the suspect purchased a weapon in furtherance of his intent to rob. This is merely an act of preparation. If a suspect enters an automobile and attempts to start the automobile by operating the ignition, etc., in a vain attempt, this is legally an attempt.[33] The activity of the suspect casing vehicles to determine the appropriate one to steal would be an act of preparation, and it would fall short of the overt act necessary to complete the attempt. If a suspect is apprehended while planting a bomb under his wife's bedroom window in an attempt to murder her, he has committed attempted murder.[34] The act of acquiring the explosive device for the purpose of murdering his wife is an act of preparation, which again falls short of the overt act required for an attempt.

Once the elements of the crime of attempt are complete, abandonment of the criminal purpose will not constitute a defense. Once the intent plus the overt act that goes beyond the mere act of preparation is complete, the defendant has satisfied the *corpus delicti* of his intentions in the furtherance of the crime itself, and his acts cannot be legally abandoned. Abandonment is a defense if the attempt to commit a crime is freely and voluntarily abandoned before the act is put in progress in final execution and when there is no outside cause prompting such abandonment.[35]

There can be no crime of attempt if there is no possibility of its consummation. If the act cannot be consummated in a legal sense because the *corpus delicti* of the crime cannot be satisfied, the impossibility of completing the crime is a valid defense. The following examples serve to explain this legal concept. If a man attempts to rape another man who is dressed in women's clothing, he is legally incapable of completing the crime from a legal point of view due to the fact that most statutes state that a female must be the object of rape.[36] If a defendant attempts to kill someone who is already dead or causes a fetus to be born dead, the defendant can probably offer the defense of impossibility of completion because in the crime of homicide, the object of the murder must be a human being. If a person attempts to shoot another with an unloaded gun, there can be no attempted crime because of the impossibility of completing the crime since the gun is incapable of projecting a missile.[37] Such a result is due to the fact that the assault with a deadly weapon statutes reflect that one must have the present ability to complete the crime, and an unloaded gun cannot fire a projectile.

An offender, however, cannot protect himself from responsibility by showing that by reason of a fact unknown to him at the time of his attempt, the crime could not have been fully carried into effect. If the *corpus delicti* of the crime can be proven, even though the act was not completed, the crime is complete. Thus, if a gambling suspect attempts to shoot a policeman whom he thinks is directly above him on the roof, but who is in reality on the other side of the roof, the *corpus delicti* of attempted murder is satisfied.[38] A defendant can be found guilty of attempting to steal money from an empty pocket because there is nothing in the crime of theft that relates to making sure that there is property for the thief to steal.[39] Also, if a doctor attempts to illegally abort a nonpregnant woman, the *corpus delicti* of illegal abortion has been satisfied.[40]

One method of sentencing on an attempt is to make it punishable in a state prison or county jail for a term not exceeding one-half the longest term of imprisonment prescribed upon a conviction of the completed offense. If the crime attempted is one in which the maximum sentence is life imprisonment or death, the guilty party may be punished by imprisonment in a state prison for a particular term, for example, not more than twenty years.

CONSPIRACY

The crime of conspiracy is the combination of two or more persons acting in concert to accomplish some criminal or unlawful purpose or to accomplish some purpose not in itself criminal or unlawful by criminal or unlawful means. In the common law, conspiracy was a misdemeanor.

The concept of conspiracy as a crime was adopted by the common-law judges from the court of the Star Chamber, which was a special court created in the sixteenth century that tried certain high crimes without a jury. An agreement made by more than one person aimed at accomplishing an unlawful objective by concerted action obviously presents a greater threat to society than do the actions of a lone offender. The purpose of the law of conspiracy is to make agreements punishable in order to prevent the commission of the substantive crimes to which they are directed before they have reached the stage of attempt. In the common law, the gist of conspiracy as a crime is the combination of minds and the agreement to accomplish some criminal or unlawful purpose. No other act other than the act of conspiring is required to constitute the crime. Modern statutes in some jurisdictions have expressly added a requirement of an overt act committed in the furtherance of the common design as a condition precedent to conspiratorial responsibility. Such an overt act need only be of comparatively slight qualitative proportions.

Conspiracy may be defined in most states as follows: If two or more persons conspire:

1. To commit any crime
2. To indict another falsely and maliciously for any crime or to procure another to be charged or arrested for any crime
3. To move or maintain falsely any suit, action or proceeding
4. To cheat and defraud any person of any property, by any means that are in themselves criminal, or to obtain money or property by false pretenses or by false promises with fraudulant intent not to perform such promises
5. To commit any act injurious to the public health, to public morals, or to pervert or obstruct justice or the due administration of the laws
6. To commit any crime against the person of the President or the Vice President of the United States, the governor of any state or territory, any United States justice or judge, or the secretary of any of the executive departments of the United States

An overt act is required to complete the crime of conspiracy; such an act must take place after the minds of the conspirators have agreed upon a particular crime. The overt act necessary is not completed by a mere meeting of the minds; it must go beyond this to the extent that at least one of the conspirators must complete some act toward the accomplishment of the purpose and object of the conspiracy.[41]

If there is a common understanding to achieve a certain purpose or to act in a certain way, a conspiracy exists without regard to whether or not there is any formal or written statement or purpose, or even if there is no actual speaking of words as to that purpose. A mere tacit understanding without any express agreement constitutes a conspiracy. The agreement may be shown by the conduct of the parties to the conspiracy. Criminal responsibility for a conspiracy is not affected by the fact that its purpose is not accomplished. It is not necessary that each conspirator know or see the others or to know all the details of the plan of operation.

A conspiracy is, in effect, a partnership in crime. To be a conspirator, a person must have criminally intended to become a party to the unlawful agreement. Mere cognizance of the commission of a crime or of the plan to commit a crime does not make the person having such knowledge a co-conspirator.

All conspiracies are felonies, and the following examples serve to explain the crime of conspiracy. If a kidnapping is planned, and the suspects station themselves outside a building to make observations in order to assist in further planning, this activity could be construed as being the overt act of the furtherance of their intent to kidnap, and thus the crime of conspiracy to kidnap is complete.[42] If funds that are to be used in carrying out a bribe are raised by more than one person, the activity of raising the funds completes the overt act and that, coupled with the intent, serves to complete the crime of conspiracy to bribe.[43] If there is an attempt to open a door in the furtherance of the intent to burglarize a building, the suspects are guilty of conspiracy to burglarize.[44]

Where a conspiracy exists, every act done by any one of the conspirators in the furtherance of the conspiracy is an act of all, even though the act was not planned or contemplated by all conspirators. Each co-conspirator is equally guilty of any consequences not anticipated, even if the conspirator was not directly involved in the particular crime. If individuals gather together to conspire to commit robbery, even if it is made quite clear that no one is to be injured or killed during the offense, if the robbery suspect who directly commits the act of burglary inadvertently kills someone in the process, each conspirator is equally guilty of murder.[45] If three people conspire to beat another person, though their intention is not to kill him, if he is killed, each individual is responsible for his death.[46] This concept regarding the position concerning an unintended act can even be stretched further. Where three persons conspire to commit robbery and send one conspirator out to purchase a weapon and in so doing, the conspirator causes the death of the proprietor of the gunshop, each conspirator is responsible for his death, even though as a group they had not contemplated killing anyone. If one conspirator commits an act that is not related to the conspiracy, he alone is responsible. For example, if three persons conspire to commit a robbery and send one conspirator out to purchase the weapon, and after purchasing the weapon, the conspirator pulls a robbery of his own that results in a death, he alone is responsible for the death.

The common-law theory that husband and wife are one made it impossible for them to be guilty of conspiracy if no third person was involved.[47] However, the *Dawson* case has been overruled, and now a husband and wife conspiring between themselves without a third party can no longer claim immunity from prosecution for conspiracy on the basis of their marital status.[48]

Unlike the crime of criminal attempt, one can withdraw from a criminal conspiracy after once having satisfied the conditions required of a co-conspirator. Acceptable guidelines that would tend to prove that a co-conspirator was conscientious in his abandonment of the conspiracy could include: 1) withdrawing from all further activity; 2) remaining away from the scene at the time the crime was committed; and 3) making his abandonment known to his co-conspirators, thus indicating his desire to entirely sever his relationship. Unless there is some affirmative act of bringing his withdrawal to the knowledge of his co-confederates, the person will be presumed to have continued in the conspiracy until the ultimate purpose of the conspiracy is achieved.[49]

The law of conspiracy was introduced to the United States in 1806 in Philadelphia, where shoemaker apprentices who called a strike for higher wages were found guilty of conspiracy. Until the 1930s, labor organizers were conspiracies favorite targets; usually they were convicted by judges and juries who found the idea of working men united for a common purpose inherently illegal. After that, the focus of the conspiracy law shifted to the communists, most of whom were accused of conspiring to advocate the overthrow of the government—a charge two steps removed from any act. In recent years, there have been a number of conspiracy trials, each one having a significant aspect in common; conspiracy charged by the prosecution and the refusal of the juries to place much credence in the government case. (E.g. U.S.V. Spock, 416F2d, conspiracy to hinder draft during the war in Viet Nam). Jurors have become confused by the conspiracy law, and in some cases, experts feel that the loose application of the conspiracy law in the hands of a zealous prosecutor can convert innocent acts, talk, and association into felonies. Noted magistrates have indicated that conspiracy laws are a prosecutor's darling and that there are tendencies toward great oppression in such a doctrine. A few magistrates feel that anyone even vaguely familiar with the law of conspiracy must soon realize that there is no crime in our system of which an innocent person can be so easily found guilty. For these reasons, the conspiracy law has not been received warmly in many courtrooms.

Endnotes

1. 14 Cal. Jur 2d, Criminal Law Sec. 4.
2. *People v. Zerillo*, 36 Cal 2d 222.
3. *People v. McLaughlin*, Ill Cal App 2d 781.
4. Restatement 2d, Tors, Sec. 282.
5. *State v. Barnett*, 63 S.E. 2d 57.
6. Perkins on Criminal Law, 2nd Ed. 759.
7. *People v. Horton*, 87 Cal Rptr 818.
8. 1 Witkin, California Crimes, Sec. 56 p. 61.
9. Perkins on Criminal Law, 2nd Ed, 751.
10. Perkins, Rollin M., *Criminal Law and Procedure*, cases and materials, Foundation Press, 1972, pg. 405.

11. *Regina v. Salisbury*, 75 Eng. Rep. 158.
12. Prosser, Transferred Intent, 1967, 45 Tex. L. Rev. 650.
13. Prosser, Law of Torts, 4th Ed. 32.
14. Bishop, Criminal Law, 8th Ed. Sec. 327.
15. Perkins on Criminal Law, 2nd Ed, 825.
16. *Regina v. Faulkner*, 13 Cox C.C. 550.
17. *Rex v. Kelly*, 1 Craw and D 186.
18. LaFave and Scott, Criminal Law, 177.
19. California Vehicle Code 20001.
20. *People v. Montecino*, 66 Cal App 2d 85.
21. *Jackson v. Commonwealth*, 38 S.W. 422.
22. *People v. Lewis*, 124 Cal 551.
23. Perkins on Criminal Law, 2nd Ed. 707.
24. *Letner v. State*, 299 S.W. 1049.
25. *People v. Cook*, 39 Mich. 236.
26. *People v. Lopez*, 254 Cal App 2d 185; Iiams v. *Superior Court*, 236 Cal App 2d 80.
27. *People v. Perrin*, 247 Cal App 2d 838; *People v. Westfall* 198 Cal App 598.
28. LaFave and Scott Criminal Law, 17.
29. Perkins on Criminal Law, 2nd Ed. 98.
30. Perkins, The Corpus Delicti of Murder; 48 Va. L. Rev. 173.
31. *People v. Bowldy*, 135 Cal App 2d 519.
32. *People v. Moran*, 18 Cal App 209.
33. *People v. Edwards*, 79 Cal 514.
34. *People v. Lanzit*, 20 Cal App 498.
35. *People v. Von Hecht*, 133 Cal App 2d 25.
36. *People v. Fratiano*, 132 Cal App 2d 610.
37. *People v. Sylvia*, 143 Cal 62.

38. *People v. Lee Kong*, 95 Cal 666.
39. *People v. Fiegelman*, 33 Cal App 2d 100.
40. *People v. Cummings*, 141 Cal App 2d 193.
41. *People v. George*, 74 Cal App 440; Cal. Penal Code § 184.
42. *People v. Stevens*, 78 Cal 395.
43. *People v. Beck*, 60 Cal App 417.
44. *People v. Rodriquez*, 61 Cal App 69.
45. *People v. Vasquez*, 49 Cal 560.
46. *People v. McMannis*, 122 Cal App 2d 891.
47. *Dawson v. United States*, 10 F. 2d 106.
48. *People v. Pierce*, 61 Cal 2d 879.
49. *People v. Moran*, 166 Cal App 2d 410.

QUESTIONS

1. Give a complete definition of *mens rea.*
2. What is negligence and how does it effect standards of legal conduct?
3. Define specific intent and apply the doctrine toward the crimes mentioned in the chapter.
4. Define malice and relate its significance toward specific intent.
5. List the elements of transferred intent and give five legal circumstances of its use.
6. What significance does the concurrence of act and intent have upon the application of the law?
7. What legal tests are usually applied to determine culpability?

8. Define *corpus delicti* and relate the rules that apply to the criminal law.
9. What are the elements of the crime of attempt?
10. What effect does the legal concept of "possibility of completion" have upon the crime of attempt? Give four examples.
11. Define conspiracy and explain how overt acts are treated differently in this crime as opposed to the crime of attempt.
12. What criminal responsibility exists for each conspirator in relation to unintended acts?

Chapter Six

CAPACITY TO COMMIT CRIME

EXEMPTIONS TO CRIMINAL LIABILITY

Under our system of justice certain classifications of individuals and states of mind are exempt from criminal liability. Criminal capacity is the mental condition which allows one to be subjected to criminal liability and legal punishment. This capacity or mental condition to commit crime is assumed to exist in everyone. Each person is presumed to have the ordinary human faculties and power to choose between right and wrong and to refrain themselves from doing that which the law forbids. Though the presumption can be rebutted, the burden of doing so is upon the defendant, who must rely on his lack of capacity as a defense and show its nonexistence by a preponderance of the evidence.

A defendant can establish lack of capacity to commit a criminal offense by showing that he is a member of a particular class which is often, by statute, deemed to lack criminal capacity.

These concepts follow the old English common-law rule of *Parens Patriae* which is concerned with the state being responsible for care of incompetents. The classifications of incompetence include children, idiots, insanity, unconsciousness, drunkeness, coverture, and ignorance or mistake of fact.

Children

Every civilized society must recognize criminal incapacity based upon extreme immaturity. A double set of standards should exist for one of very tender years who has committed a criminal or negligent act. There is a difference of opinion among the various states as to what this double set of standards should be in terms of age. According to common law, a child under the age of seven had no criminal capacity. Up to age fourteen there was also a rebuttable presumption of incapacity, regarding one so young he may not comprehend the significance of the criminal act. The common law permits the criminal conviction of a child between these ages but only upon clear proof that the child could establish an appreciation or understanding of the wrongfulness of the act. One who has reached the age of fourteen had criminal capacity unless incapacity was established on an entirely different basis, such as insanity.

The age, below which there is complete criminal incapacity, has been raised by statutes in some jurisdictions. Thus, it has been placed at eight in England, at nine in Texas, ten in Georgia, and at twelve in Arkansas. Furthermore, the net result of some of the juvenile delinquency statutes is to raise it much higher.[1] Such age is omitted entirely from some statutes; for example, California provides in substance that children under the age of fourteen are incapable of crime in the absence of clear proof that they knew its wrongfulness at the time of commiting the act charged against them.

Juveniles have been treated under a process separate from adult courts for many years. The state of Illinois began the process by setting up a separate set of standards and procedures for juveniles in 1899. California followed shortly thereafter with its set of standards in 1903, and Wyoming was the last state to treat juveniles differently by legislation enacted in 1945.

Idiots

Idiot is a term used to describe one born with practically no intellectual or social awareness. In terms of the Binet classification, the IQ of an idiot ranges between 0 and 24.

Idiots are incapable of committing crimes. However, the practical problem of determining what idiocy is has greatly narrowed the classification. Low mentality alone has not been sufficient, nor has extreme feeblemindedness. The courts seem to lean toward a right-wrong test when all else fails. The defendant's mentality must be so low as to preclude any distinction between right and wrong. If the defendant passes such a test, he is deemed a "legal idiot" and will not be held accountable for his actions.

Insanity

Insanity is a term to which numerous definitions are attached, and these vary with different perspectives or frames of reference. The medical profession has its various views, layman have their own ideas, and courts of law are confused. Here, we are concerned with legal insanity and not medical insanity.

The question of insanity becomes important at the following points in a criminal case.

1. At the time of the alleged crime, the defendant was laboring under such a defect of reason, from disease of the mind, as to be incapable of knowing the nature and significance of his acts, he will be entitled to an acquittal.
2. If at the arraignment he is so disordered by mental disease that he is unable to plead intelligently, he should not be permitted to plea until his reason is restored.
3. At any point in the criminal proceedings, if the defendant because of mental disease is unable to understand the charges against him and the possible defenses thereto, and unable to counsel with his attorney in regard to the conduct of the trial, he ought not to be tried at that particular time whether or not he was insane or sane at the time of the alleged crime.
4. If, after the defendant is tried and found guilty, he is unable to appreciate the wrongfulness of his acts by reason of a degree of mental defect or disease before judgment, judgment shall not be pronounced.

In summary, an insane person cannot plead to an indictment, be subjected to trial, have judgments pronounced against him, or undergo punishment. A valid indictment may be found against him but no further proceedings can be had if he is insane at the time.[2] The case remains in limbo while the defendant receives psychiatric treatment. When an accused is found to be insane at the time of the alleged offense, he must be acquitted. Various tests, rules, or definitions of insanity have been formulated over the years.

Most state courts and federal courts utilize the M'Naghten rule as the test of insanity. Daniel M'Naghten attempted to kill Sir Robert Peel in England in 1843 but instead killed Edward Drummand. The case reflects that a defendant is not entitled to a defense on the ground of insanity unless at the time he was laboring under such a defect of reason, from disease of the mind, as not to know the nature and quality of the act he was committing; or, if he did know it, that he did not know what he was doing was wrong. This is the so called, right-wrong test of insanity or the M'Naghten rule. (M'Naghten Case, 10 Clark and F. 200; 8 Eng. Rep. R 718).

Four points stand out and should be understood whenever reference to M'Naghten is made.

1. It applies only in case of "a defect of reason, from disease of the mind." This includes congenital defect as well as physical trauma.
2. If, because of this "defect of reason", the defendant did not know what he was doing, he is not guilty of the crime.
3. If he knew what he was doing, he is not guilty if he did not know he was doing wrong.

4. If the defendant acted under an insane delusion, his accountability to the criminal law is the same as if the facts were as they seemed to him.[3]

The essence of M'Naghten is that the mental disease or incapacitating defect must be of such a degree as to leave the person irrational, that is, no rational person lacks criminal capacity by reason of insanity.[4] The M'Naghten rule has been found by various courts to be inadequate as an exclusive criterion of insanity. Some say it does not take sufficient account of psychic realities and scientific knowledge, while others claim it is based upon a symptom and so cannot validly be applied in all circumstances.[5] There is no graduating scale of insanity with the M'Naghten rule (right-wrong test), only a finding of total insanity or total sanity at the time the act was committed. Due to this fact some courts have abandoned the M'Naghten rule for more contemporary tests of insanity.

One such court was the second United States Court of Appeals which in 1966 replaced the M'Naghten rule with a more liberal formula. The court (in United States v. Freeman 357, F 2d, 606) indicated that "M'Naghten does not comply with modern medical knowledge that an individual is a mentally complex being with varying degrees of awareness. It fails to attack the problem where the accused may have understood his actions, but was incapable of controlling his actions." The court's decision affects federal courts in nine western states and the territory of Guam.

The "irresistible impulse" test of insanity has

been recognized by the Supreme Court of the United States as a defense. The "irresistible impulse" test of insanity is provided as a ground of partial excuse in the case of homicide committed under the emotional state of provocation. In such jurisdictions, notwithstanding that one accused of crime may have been able to comprehend the nature and consequences of his act, and to know that it was wrong, if he was forced to its execution by an impulse which he was powerless to control as a consequence of an actual disease of the mind, he will be excused. If the impulse is based upon emotion, moral insanity, instability, passion, or anger, rather than a diseased mental condition, the irresistible impulse is no defense. Whether an impulse in a given case is irresistible is a question for the jury.

The United States Court of Appeals in *Durham* v. *United States* cast aside the irresistible-impulse test indicating that, like the M'Naghten rule, it was also inadequate in that it gave no recognition to mental illness characterized by brooding and reflection and so relegates acts caused by such illness to the application of the inadequate right-wrong test.

The Durham Rule (*Durham* v. *United States,* 214 F. 2d, 862) was enunciated in 1954 by the Federal Court of Appeals for the District of Columbia.

The court stated it as follows: It is simply that the accused is not criminally responsible if his unlawful act was the product of mental disease or mental defect. We use disease in the sense of a condition that is capable of either improving or deteriorating. We use, "defect" in the sense of a condition that is not considered capable of improving or deteriorating and which may be either congenital, or the result of injury, or the residual effect of a physical or mental disease. Any future instructions to a jury must in some way convey the sense and substance of the following: "If you the jury believe, beyond a reasonable doubt, that the accused was not suffering from a diseased or defective mental condition at the time he committed the criminal act charged, you may find him guilty. If you believe he was suffering from a diseased or defective mental condition when he commited the act, but believed, beyond a reasonable doubt that the act was not the product of such mental abnormality, you may find him guilty. Unless you believe, beyond a reasonable doubt, either that he was not suffering from a diseased or defective mental condition, or that the act was the product of such abnormality, you must find the accused not guilty by reason of insanity."

The Model Penal Code in section 4.01 provides still another definition. The code indicates that a person is not responsible for criminal conduct if at the time of such conduct, as a result of mental disease or defect, he lacks substantial capacity either to appreciate the criminality (wrongfulness) of his conduct or to conform his conduct to the requirements of law.

Diminished Capacity

"Diminished capacity," sometimes called "partial insanity," is a concept arising in the regular trial part of criminal proceedings. (It does not result in a separate trial as a straight insanity defense does.)

The test of diminished capacity stems from two

propositions of criminal law. First, to be guilty of a crime the defendant must commit a criminal act. Second, when the act was committed, the defendant must have harbored a specific criminal intent. The defendant is not guilty of murder merely because of the act of pulling the trigger. He must also intend to kill. That is why an individual can be seen to kill the victim (the act) by a multitude of witnesses and yet be found guilty of a lesser offense because of an inability to establish the requisite mental state.

This is how it works. Most state statutes define murder as the:

1) Unlawful killing of a human being
2) With malice aforethought

If the D.A. can establish the first but not the second because of diminished capacity, then voluntary manslaughter will be the verdict.

The advantage of diminished capacity over a plea of not guilty by reason of insanity is that a person found insane may be committed to an institution for perhaps the rest of his life; yet a person found to have a diminished capacity for formulating a specific mental state may receive straight probation or a very light sentence. Such is not necessarily a bad result. Most people feel that an alcoholic should not be punished like a regular burglar if he breaks a door on a closed business, goes inside, and passes out.

People v. *Conley*, 64 Cal. 2d. 310, is an important case discussing diminished capacity and giving definitions concerning its application. This case, which dealt mostly with court instructions, attempted to differentiate and define elements of guilt under diminished capacity in homicide cases.

For example, murder is the unlawful killing of a human being with malice aforethought. Malice aforethought, as used in the context of the defense of diminished capacity, means that a person is capable of achieving such a mental state that he is normally capable of comprehending the duties society places on all persons to act within the law. If, despite such awareness, he commits an act likely to cause serious injury or death to another, and if he exhibits wanton disregard for human life or antisocial motivation, then malice aforethought is present.

Malice aforethought, either expressed or implied, therefore, is manifested by the commission of an act by a person who is able to comprehend prohibition of this act by society, and has an obligation to conform his conduct to society's rules. If because of mental illness, mental defect, or intoxication, the defendant does not have the capacity to harbor malice as defined, he cannot be found guilty of murder (which requires malice). He could be convicted of voluntary or involuntary manslaughter which does not require malice.

If the murder is perpetrated by any kind of willful, deliberate premeditation, it is of the first degree. If because of mental illness, defect, or intoxication the defendant could not deliberate or premeditate at the time the murder was committed, he cannot be found guilty of an offense greater than that of second degree murder. Courts have reflected that under the Wells-Gorshen rule of diminished capacity, even though a defendant is legally sane according to the M'Naghten test, if he was suffering from a mental illness that prevented his acting with malice aforethought or with premeditation and deliberation, he cannot be convicted of murder in the first degree.[6]

Psychiatrist Bernard L. Diamond reflects on the diminished capacity rule: "It eliminates the all or none business of an insanity rule. It takes into account the whole range of mental illness, from mild to severe and relates them to the fine graduation that exists in criminal law for dealing with the guilty mind. If a defendant cannot properly reflect upon malice, premeditation or deliberation, this will lessen his degree of criminal responsibility."[7]

Diminished capacity has importance in *any* crime which requires a specific, well defined mental intent, such as—

1. Assault with intent to commit murder or rape;
2. Burglary (entry with intent to commit theft or other unlawful act);
3. Theft (intent to defraud or permanently deprive the victim of his property).

The following are examples where diminished capacity is applied. 1) Defendant killed his foreman after extremely heavy drinking. He was allowed to prove the heavy drinking as well as the fact he was a chronic paranoid schizophrenic. Such evidence could reduce the conviction to manslaughter.[8] 2) Defendant, who had been drinking for three days and taking pain medication, shot and killed his girlfriend and her husband. Defendant said he remembered nothing about what happened. A psychiatrist said all this caused him to be different from his normal personality. The judge was required to give the jury the option of finding him guilty of manslaughter rather than murder.

Unconsciousness

It has been generally stated that if a person was unconscious and unaware of what he was doing, no degree of criminality can attach thereto. This rule applies only to cases of the unconsciousness of persons of sound mind, for example, somnambulists or persons suffering from delirium of fever, epilepsy, a blow on the head, or the involuntary taking of drugs or intoxicating liquor, and other cases in which there is no functioning of the conscious mind and the person's acts are controlled solely by the subconscious mind.

An act done in the absence of the will is not any more the behavior of the actor than is an act done contrary to his will. Unconsciousness, so long as it is not voluntarily induced such as by intoxication is, therefore, a complete defense to a criminal charge.

Ignorance or Mistake of Fact

The time worn expression, ignorance of the law is no excuse, is a valid legal concept. For example, ignorance of the law is no excuse because the law is written down for all to see. Every person is presumed to know the law. This concept is not entirely without exception, although the exceptions are rare.

At the common law, ignorance or mistake of fact on the part of the accused, at least if reasonable and not due to carelessness or negligence, is a defense. Since criminal intent is the essence of any true offense, when a person without fault or carelessness is misled concerning facts and acts as he would be justified in doing were the facts what he believed them to be, he is legally innocent. Such an honest mistake of fact excuses the otherwise criminal act which it prompts. His trial proceeds on the fiction that the facts were as he mistakenly supposed them to be and not as they really were. In order to substantiate a crime, there must be a union of act and intent, or criminal negligence. If one is to offset criminal responsibility utilizing the defense of ignorance or mistake of fact, he must agree that he committed the criminal act but argue that it was without criminal intent or negligence.

Thus, it is no crime for a person to assault another person whom he reasonably, though mistakenly, believes to be committing a burglary; or for a person, intending to kill a burglar in his own home, to kill by mistake a member of his own family; or for a person to take a coat from a restaurant rack, mistakenly believing it to be his own; or for a person to pass counterfeit money when he believes it to be genuine; or for a person to join an illegal conspiracy while being ignorant of its true character; or for a male to have unlawful sexual intercourse with a female who is under the age of consent when he believes her to be of age.

The accused has the burden of producing evidence that he was honestly mistaken as to the facts and his conduct was prompted by a mistake. He must, in other words, convince the members of the jury that he is telling the truth when he says he made a mistake.

It is further noted that under many modern statutes which impose strict liability upon a person who commits a prohibited act, regardless of his state of mind, ignorance or mistake of fact may not be a defense. Acts not evil in themselves but prohibited by the statute are not excused by ignorance or mistake of fact where they are made punishable irrespective of intent or motive. Thus, knowledge of the age of the person named in the complaint is not essential to the violation of a statute forbiding the manager of a dance hall to permit any person under the age of twenty-one to be there when such knowledge is not required by the statute. Even a well-grounded mistake of fact is not exculpatory in this area of the law if the mistake could have been discovered by the use of a degree of care which it is not unreasonable to require of one in a particular situation. Such statutes, deemed necessary for the common good, require persons to ascertain the true facts for themselves.

The Model Penal Code states:

> 1. Section 2.04. Ignorance or mistake as to a matter of fact or law is a defense if;
>
> a. Ignorance of mistake negatives the purpose, knowledge, belief, recklessness or negligence required to establish a material element of the defense;
>
> b. The law provides that the state of mind established by such ignorance of mistake constitutes a defense.
>
> 2. Although ignorance or mistake would otherwise afford a defense to the

offense charged the defense is not available if the defendant would be guilty of another offense had the situation been as he supposed. In such cases, however, the ignorance or mistake of the defendant shall reduce the grade and degree of the offense of which he may be convicted to those of the offense of which he would be guilty had the situation been how he supposed.

Coverture (Marital Coercion)

At common law, it was presumed, that crimes committed by a married woman in her husband's presence were committed under his coercion (except for the crimes of murder and treason). This presumption is rebuttable and is on the wane, although it has not disappeared entirely. At common law, a married woman was otherwise responsible for her individual crimes.

Many states recognize coverture as a defense for criminal liability. "A married woman is not capable of committing a misdemeanor while acting under threats, command or coercion of her husband."[9]

Compulsion

When an act is done from compulsion or necessity, it generally cannot be a crime where the compulsion or necessity is clear and conclusive, and arose without negligence or fault on the part of the accused. To constitute a defense, the coercion involved must be present, imminent, impending, and of such a nature as to induce a well-grounded fear of death or serious bodily injury if the act is not done. There must be no opportunity for escape, or fear of remote or slight personal injury; mere loss of property is no excuse. Thus, if a man at the point of a bank robber's gun under the threat of immediate death is ordered to drive the getaway car he is obviously not punishable for the bank robbery. The question of what acts are sufficient to constitute compulsion is one for the jury.

Although compulsion is a defense in the case of most crimes, it will not justify taking the life of an innocent person. The law will not excuse the intentional killing of an innocent person on the plea that it was necessary to save the life of the accused, no matter how great the necessity. Moreover, economic necessity is not a justification for larceny and will not excuse the theft of another person's property. Furthermore, there is a defense to criminal liability when a person is forced to commit a crime (excluding crimes which provide for the death penalty) by being subjected to threats of great and imminent danger to their lives.

FORMER JEOPARDY OR DOUBLE JEOPARDY

Exemption from criminal liability includes those who have already been through another trial for the same offense. The Fifth Amendment to the United

States Constitution states in part, " . . . nor shall any person be subject for the same offense to be twice put in jeopardy of life or limb." It seems fundamental to the sense of fair play and justice that the state should not be able to retry a defendant on the same charges again after he has been once acquitted. Were it otherwise, each of the other constitutionally guaranteed procedural safeguards would be but an empty mockery, for any procedural blunders made by the state at the first trial could be remedied at the second trial, the third, or the fourth. If the notion of former jeopardy meant only that the defendant could not be tried several times for the identical crime, the courts would not have much difficulty, but as one may see, much more is at stake.

At the onset, before exploring the many facets of this notion of former jeopardy it might be well to see how it relates to the concept of included offenses. An excellent indicator of the similarities and contrasts of these two concepts is the following criminal statute, which states that:

> . . . an act or omission which is made punishable in different ways by different provisions of this code may be punished under either of such provisions, but in no case can it be punished under more than one; an acquittal or conviction and sentence under either one bars a prosecution for the same act or omission under any other.

In *People* v. *Tideman* (1962) 57 C. 2d 574, the court, in discussing this theory stated:

> Thus it is established that the statute prohibits multiple punishments for a single act, but like the jeopardy doctrine, has no application to multiple convictions as such, in a single prosecution. It does by its carefully chosen language, extend its reach to prohibit subsequent prosecution for the same act or omission, and this, of course, would encompass a lesser offense necessarily included in such 'act or omission.' In this application the effect of the statute would resemble the protection of the jeopardy doctrine but with this important difference: the statute becomes available only after there has been 'an acquittal or conviction and sentence.' The shield of the statute does not follow from mere jeopardy. The conjunction of 'conviction and sentence' makes altogether clear the legislative intention that punishment or acquittal, not mere jeopardy, is the essential requirement for the operation of this section.

The court's foregoing decision enunciates these points of law.

1. This theory of law, like the former jeopardy doctrine and like the included offenses doctrine does not preclude multiple convictions under various code sections for multiple crimes arising from a single act by the defendant, *in a single prosecution.*
2. This theory does prohibit the state from prosecuting a second time for the same act or omission after the first trial has ended in

> conviction or acquittal. This states one facet of the doctrine of included offenses. The doctrine of former jeopardy would prevent a second trial after jeopardy had attached, which would occur, in most cases, before the stage of conviction or acquittal.

So the major thrust of the doctrine of double jeopardy is to prevent multiple prosecutions for the same act or offense and the main effect of the doctrine of included offenses is to prevent multiple punishments for the same act or offense in a single trial.

What Is Jeopardy?

By way of definition, it would be helpful to discuss some instances where the doctrine of former jeopardy has no application, that is, an administrative proceeding and later criminal prosecution or vice versa.

Consider these hypothetical facts. A police officer, due to his gross negligence and general lack of attentiveness, fires his weapon and kills a fellow police officer. He is forthwith discharged from the force after an administrative hearing that determines his guilt beyond a reasonable doubt. The District Attorney then charges this officer with manslaughter. Will his plea of former jeopardy (in the administrative hearing) be a bar to the criminal prosecution? The answer is no. Although the officer can argue persuasively that not only was he formerly put in jeopardy for the same offense, he was also convicted and punished, therefore the argument has no merit as it is quite beside the point. As a general rule, administrative sanctions are not construed to constitute the sort of jeopardy that will bar a subsequent criminal prosecution, and this proposition has a sound basis in common sense. Were the contrary true, the aforementioned officer would be immune from criminal prosecution because he had been fired from his job, or, conversely, he could not be fired from his job if first he were convicted in a criminal court. Either circumstance would indeed be ridiculous. The same principle would apply to the lawyer guilty of forgery who was disbarred and later convicted in a criminal court, or the doctor guilty of criminal abortion whose license had been revoked and who was subsequently convicted in a court of law.

Multiple Convictions in a Single Trial

If one does an act that constitutes two or more crimes in a single jurisdiction, that is, by clubbing a victim to death one commits both murder and battery, and is convicted of both in a single trial, the doctrine of former jeopardy would have no application as it applies only to successive trials for the same offense. However, on the above facts the doctrine of included offenses would most likely apply.

Single Act or Offense That Is Made a Crime in Two or More Jurisdictions

It is possible that one may do an act that may be a crime in two states; a crime against both a state and the federal government; or against a state, the federal government, and a foreign government. Is the attachment of jeopardy or conviction or acquittal in one jurisdiction a bar to prosecution in another by virtue of the doctrine of former jeopardy? The answer generally is no. Consider these facts. A person places a bomb on a plane in New York, the bomb explodes as the airliner lands in Mexico City, killing all passengers aboard and some Mexican citizens who were awaiting the arrival of the plane. The bomber is most likely, by his single act of placing a bomb on a plane, guilty of murder in New York, Mexico, and under United States Federal law. And he could be convicted in any one, two, or three of the jurisdictions. He has, by a single act, transgressed against three sovereign powers and is accountable to each. Some states, however, allow this to be used as a defense. As an example, one criminal statute states:

> Whenever on the trial of an accused person it appears that upon a criminal prosecution under the laws of another state, government, or country, founded upon the act or commission in respect to which he is on trial, he has been acquitted or convicted, it is a sufficient defense.

As a further example, another criminal statute states:

> When an act charged as a public offense is within the jurisdiction of another state

> or country, as well as of this state, a conviction or acquittal thereof in the former is a bar to the prosecution or indictment therefore in this state.

Two observations should be made regarding the two statutes:

1. Both apply only where the prior prosecution in another jurisdiction has terminated in a conviction or acquittal and do not apply where the trial has been terminated in some other manner after jeopardy has attached.
2. Neither code section, of course, would be a bar to a prosecution in another jurisdiction subsequent to a prosecution in the initial jurisdiction.

The Single Act with Multiple Victims in a Single Jurisdiction

A man, with malice and premeditation, sets fire to his home intending to kill his wife and two children. His expectations are realized. Normally the state would prosecute all three murders in a single trial because all of the items of proof are the same. That is to say, if the act of setting the house afire is proved for one murder, it is proved for all, and, if the mental state of malice is proved for one, it is proved for all.

But suppose that the state opted for separate

prosecutions and the defendant is convicted of killing his wife and given life imprisonment. He is then, in a second trial, convicted of killing one child and given a life sentence, but upon being convicted of killing the other child in a third trial he is given the death penalty. In a case almost identical to the aforementioned example the court in *Cicucci* v. *Illinois*, (1958) 356 U.S. 464, held such successive trials to be valid.

After seeing the fact situations to which the doctrine of former jeopardy has no applicability, consider the elements of the doctrine and some of its applications. For the doctrine of former jeopardy to have any application, it is basic that the defendant must have been placed in jeopardy in a former trial. One is placed in jeopardy when brought to trial—

1. by a valid indictment or information;
2. before a court of competent jurisdiction (i.e., jurisdiction over both the defendant and the offense);
3. before a jury duly sworn and instructed or before a judge.

In a jury trial, jeopardy attaches when the jury is sworn; in a court trial, it attaches when the first witness is sworn. As a general statement of the rule, one may not be tried on any successive occasion after jeopardy has attached in a prior trial, regardless of the outcome of that prior trial. There are, however, some exceptions to that general rule. In the following instances, jeopardy, although once attached, would be deemed waived or at least would not be a bar to a subsequent prosecution.

1. When, through the fault of no one, it becomes impossible to continue the trial and a mistrial is called because:
   a. The judge becomes incapacitated and unable to continue the trial.
   b. The defendant is unable, through sickness or otherwise, to continue.
   c. A juror is unable to continue and for some reason an alternate cannot be seated.
   d. The jury is unable to reach a verdict.
2. When, because of misconduct by the defendant, the trial is unable to continue.
3. When the defendant has had a conviction set aside by appeal or other means. But, generally, the defendant may only be retried for the same offense and not either a higher crime arising out of the same act or a higher degree of the same crime. Also, as a general proposition, the defendant may not receive a harsher sentence at the second trial, but in unique fact situations this rule may not apply.

The doctrine of former jeopardy states that one may not be tried twice for the same *offense;* the courts, however, have had difficulty determining just how to define the same offense. Courts in various jurisdictions have devised certain tests to determine just what constitutes the same offense. Some of the more common tests are—

1. *the evidence test:* If the same evidence is used to prove both the first and second offense, then both are the same offense.

2. *the act-intent test:* If defendant, by one act, and with identical intent commits two offenses, the offenses are the same even though there are multiple victims.
3. *the same offense in law and fact test:* Both offenses must be the same in both law and fact, if either offense is different in either, it may be prosecuted independently. But note, if the facts are identical, even though the offenses are different in law and the doctrine of double jeopardy would not bar a subsequent prosecution, it is unlikely that the defendant could be punished for both.

MOTIVE

Over the years some naive people have thought that a person cannot be prosecuted when motive cannot be determined. Such is clearly not true. Motive is to be distinguished from intent in the criminal law as the desire or inducement which tempts or prompts a person to commit a criminal act. Intent is a person's resolve or purpose to do the criminal act, whereas motive is the reason which leads the mind to desire a certain result. Intent is the determination to use a particular means to affect that result. The motive may be a desire to injure or to benefit. A person may want to kill another out of hatred, revenge, jealousy, or fear in the usual murder case. However, in a mercy killing, the motive that prompted his intent to cause the victim's death may have been love. It is important to distinguish between the basic urge itself and the intent which resulted in the mind of the particular person, but which might not have been generated in the mind of another. When, for example, it is said that a legatee, who was aware of a large bequest in his favor, had a motive for killing his deceased testator, it is not meant that this fact is sufficient to establish an intent to kill. That this fact was sufficient to generate a primitive urge of that bind, although it might be completely checked, is all that is meant.

Motive is not an essential element of crime.[10] Sometimes the statement is even more positive in form: Motive is never an essential element to a crime.[11] Proof of motive is never necessary to support a conclusion of guilt otherwise sufficiently established.[12] A person is not to be acquitted simply because his motive for committing a crime cannot be discovered. If the commission of a crime accompanied by the requisite criminal intent is clearly proved, all the requisites of guilt have been established. The basic urge that led his mind to desire the result forbidden by the law which he accomplished is immaterial.

Proof of motive may be clearly relevant and is always admissible on behalf of the prosecution or of the defendant; it is especially pertinent where the evidence in a case is circumstancial.

INTOXICATION

At early common law, voluntary intoxication did not excuse the commission of crime. In fact, intoxication actually aggravated guilt because it was morally and legally wrong. Since the 19th century, however, this strict rule has been modified. Today, the fact of voluntary intoxication is generally not a defense and does not in itself affect the capacity of a person to commit a crime, nor his legal responsibility for it. The fact that alcohol may have inflammed the passions of the accused, reduced his self-control, or increased his boldness is no excuse. Thus, the fact that the mental state to kill is conceived in a mind excited by drink is no defense in a prosecution for homicide. It is immaterial in a prosecution for involuntary manslaughter by drunken driving that the accused was so intoxicated that he could not realize that he might kill another.

If a specific mental state is an element of an offense, however, and the accused intoxication negates its existence, his intoxication may be a defense. For example, it is a defense to show that the accused was too drunk to entertain the intent to commit a felony in burglary of a dwelling house at night so as to be guilty of entering a house with the intention of committing theft or some felony. (See diminished capacity, p. 154.) Furthermore, if, in fact, the use of intoxicants has made an accused permanently insane, his capacity is determined by the usual rules applicable to insane persons, and it is immaterial that his condition was created by the voluntary use of intoxicants.

Involuntary intoxication—that produced by the fraud or coercion of another—may be a defense under the circumstances of a particular case. If a temporary insanity is produced thereby, it is treated the same as permanent insanity.

The Model Penal Code under section 2.28 relates—

1. Except as provided in subsection 4 of this section, intoxication of the actor is not a defense unless it negates an element of the defense;
2. When recklessness establishes an element of the offense, if the actor, due to the self-induced intoxication, is unaware of a risk of which he would have been aware if he had been sober, unawareness is immaterial;
3. Intoxication does not, in itself, constitute mental disease within the meaning of section 4.01.
4. Intoxication which
   a. is not self induced, or
   b. is pathological is an affirmative defense if by reason of such intoxication the actor, at the time of his conduct, lacks substantial capacity either to appreciate its criminality or to conform his conduct to the requirements of the law.
5. Definitions. In this section unless a different meaning plainly is required;
   a. Intoxication means a disturbance of mental or physical capacities resulting from the introduction of substances into the body;
   b. Self-induced intoxication means intoxication caused by substances which the actor knowingly introduces into his body, the tendency of which to cause intoxication he knows or ought to know, unless he introduces pursuant to medical advice or under such circumstances as would afford a defense to a charge of crime;

c. Pathological intoxication means intoxication grossly excessive in degree, given the amount of the intoxicant to which the actor does not know he is susceptible.

If the offense charged requires a specific intent, the defendant is not guilty if he was too intoxicated at the time to have any such intent, and had not entertained such an intent prior to his intoxication. One who drinks to nerve himself to commit a crime already decided upon, and who thereupon does commit that crime, is not in a position to maintain that he was too drunk at the time to entertain the intent which he executed.[13] If, for example, a defendant is charged with burglary, and the accusatory pleading reflects that A broke into the dwelling house of B with the intent to steal and the evidence shows that A opened the front door of B's house late at night, went in, and was found in a drunken stupor on the floor, such a finding will not support a conviction of burglary.[14] A fumbling effort to gain entry into a building by one too drunk to be capable of entertaining any intent is not an attempt to commit burglary.[15] If a defendant is too drunk to entertain a specific intent to murder, he is not guilty of an assault with intent to kill.[16]

PARTIES TO A CRIME

A person may have the capacity to commit a crime even though he himself does not perform the prohibited act. In crimes involving more than one person, there are varying degrees of involvement. Therefore, on those individuals the law confirms a title which corresponds to their participation in a crime. At the common law those who participated in crime were generally considered to be either principals or accessories depending upon the prominence of their role and its commission. This distinction, however, was recognized only in felony cases. As to both treason and misdemeanor, all who shared in them were deemed to be principals. This was because treason was so heinious in its nature, there could be no varying shades of guilt, while misdemeanor offenses were not so abhorrent, a formal distinction between those who had a hand in them was not felt to be worthwhile.

Today, the importance of the statutes in their different jurisdictions is great in regard to the parties to crime, and their language and interpretation by the courts must be carefully studied. The parties to a felony at common law fell into the following categories.

1. Principals in the first degree
2. Principals in the second degree
3. Accessories before the fact
4. Accessories after the fact

Generally, a principal in the first degree is the actual offender who commits the criminal act. If he uses an innocent agent, however, he is still the real offender and, thus, a principal in the first degree. His presence at the scene of the crime is not essential for he may start a chain of events which causes a harm in his absence; for example, the principal plants a bomb which will explode later. There may be more than one principal in the first degree in a particular crime; for example, two persons committing a strong arm robbery on the person of another.

A principal in the second degree is one who, with knowledge of what is afoot, aids and abets the principal in the first degree at the very time the felony is committed by rendering him aid, assistance, or encouragement. Such an aider or abettor is always equally punishable with the actual doer of the deed at common law. He must be present at the scene of the crime or at a convenient distance. When a lookout, a typical principal in the second degree, is situated in a position to give assistance to the perpetrator at the moment the offense is committed, he is said to be constructively present.

The law of accessories, developed at a time when most felonies were punishable by death and statutes, had made felonies out of a multitude of misdeeds which were not considered sufficiently grave to merit such extreme penalties. Thus, the law of accessories operated as a device to reduce the number of capital convictions by providing handicaps to the prosecution in regard to the subjects of jurisdictions, pleading, trial, and guilt. For example, an accessory could not be forced to trial before the trial of the principal. Hence, if the principal was never apprehended, there was no possibility of convicting the accessory.

An accessory before the fact is a person who, before a crime is committed, knows that the particular offense has been contemplated, assents to or approves of it, and expresses his view of it in a form which operates to encourage the principal to perform the deed. However, he must be too far away to actually aid in the felonious act. There is a close resemblance between an accessory before the fact and a principal in the second degree. The same counsel, command, encouragement, or aid which will make a person present at the moment of perpetration, a principal in the second degree, will make him an accessory before the fact if he is absent.

It is immaterial whether or not the principal commits the crime in the manner counseled by the accessory. As long as the crime is committed, the advisor is guilty as an accessory before the fact if there is an immediate casual connection between the instigation and the act. Mere knowledge of a contemplated crime, without evidence of intentional encouragement, will not make a person an accessory before the fact. Mere concealment of knowledge that a felony is to be committed does not make the party concealing it an accessory before the fact.

An accessory after the fact is one who, knowing that a person has committed a felony, aids the felon into escape in any way or prevents his arrest and prosecution. He may help the felon elude justice, for example, by concealing, sheltering, relieving, or comforting him while he is a fugitive; by supplying him with a means of escape; or by destroying dangerous evidence. Thus, the accessory after the fact stands in a more remote degree of complicity than the other parties to crime. His offense is dependant on the fact of the felony involved that is a distinct and separate crime. One who would be an accessory after the fact in a felony case would be a principal in a treason case, but such a person is not regarded as a guilty party and is not criminally responsible if the offense involved is a misdemeanor.

An accessory after the fact in a felony case must have an intention to assist the felon and must actually do so. Mere knowledge that a person has committed a felony and failure to inform the authorities of that fact does not make a person an accessory after the fact at common law. One who merely abstains, however willfully, from arresting a known felon, and allows him to make his escape, is not an accessory after the fact. Such conduct, however, may make a person guilty of an independant substitute offense such as misprision.

At common law, a wife incurs no liability if she hides her fugitive husband since it was considered a wife's duty to aid him and keep his secrets. Special statutory provisions, however, may change this rule. At common law, there was no similar exemption from liability if a husband assisted his felon wife, and he became an accessory to her crime.

Although, historically, an accessory after the fact was punished the same as a principal, in contemporary times a much more lenient punishment is imposed upon those who are accessories after the fact than is imposed upon the other parties to crime. Presently, under many statutes, the distinction between principals in the first and second degree is not of much practical importance, and in some instances has been entirely abolished. For example, the federal law provided that whoever commits an offense or aids, abets, counsels, commands, induces, or procures its commission is a principal, and, that whoever causes an act to be done which, if directly performed by him would be a crime, is also a principal and punishable as such. Furthermore, statutes in some states have abolished the common-law distinction between a principal and an accessory before the fact, and they provide that the latter may be indicted, tried, and convicted as a principal. In a number of states the distinction, either expressed or implied, is preserved. But, at the same time, it is commonly provided that the punishment is the same for both offenders.

The distinction between a principal in the second degree and an accessory before the fact, it will be observed, was founded upon the presence or the nonpresence at the commission of the crime of the party aiding and abetting the perpetrator of the act which constituted the final consummation of the crime in its commission. Undoubtedly, the legislature thus viewed the proposition and, therefore, by express mandate, has abrogated the mere formal distinction existing at common law between principals in the commission of crimes and accessories before the fact, or those participating in their commission without actually perpetrating the acts which, with the intent, constitute the crime. Therefore, whatever may be the law in other jurisdictions, the rule in California as laid down by the legislature is that "all persons concerned in a commission of a crime, whether it be a felony or misdemeanor, and whether they directly commit the act constituting the offense, or aid and abet in its commission, or, not being present, have advised and encouraged its commission, are principals in any crime so committed and would be prosecuted, as principals, and no other facts need be alleged."[17]

As a further example, state statutes generally relate that the distinction between an accessory before the fact and a principal, and between principals in the first and second degrees, is abrogated whether the crime be felony or misdemeanor, and all persons concerned in the commission of the crime, whether they directly commit the act constituting the offense, or aid and abet in its commission, though not present, shall thereafter be prosecuted, tried, and punished as principals, and no other facts need be alleged in any indictment or information against such an accessory than are required in an indictment or information against the principal.

The definition of one who directly commits the act is self-explanatory: the one who actually steals the merchandise or the one who actually renders the victim deceased, for example. The classification of individuals who aid and abet in the commission of a crime is somewhat more complicated. To aid is defined as to give support, help, assistance, and so on, and does not necessarily imply knowledge. To abet implies knowledge of wrongful purpose. In order for one to be classified as a principal he must both aid and abet the crime because to aid without knowledge is not a crime. For example, if a cab driver picks up his fare and transports the fare to a liquor store, whereupon the fare holds up the liquor store without the prior knowledge of the cab driver, and after transporting the fare to another location the cab driver is arrested for robbery, he is not a principal to the crime.[18] He aided in the crime; however, he did not abet the crime. The following are examples of occurrences wherein individuals are classified as principals because they aided and abetted.

1. The wheelman acting as a lookout or driving the getaway car in a robbery
2. A mother is guilty of rape after assisting her boyfriend in the rape of her daughter
3. A husband is guilty of raping his wife if he

forces his wife to have intercourse with his best friend

4. A passenger inside of a vehicle who urges and assists the driver of the vehicle to commit hit and run could be guilty of aiding and abetting the crime

The third type of principal is the person who, with knowledge that an illegal act is going to transpire, advises and encourages the commission of the crime, but is not present at the scene of the crime. Formerly, under common law, this type of principal was called an accessory before the fact.

As was previously mentioned, under common law, an accessory after the fact was defined as an individual who, after a felony had been committed, harbors, conceals, or aids a principal in such a felony with the intent that said principal may escape from arrest, trial, conviction, or punishment, having knowledge that said principal has committed such felony or has been charged with such a felony. Most states have dropped the accessory after the fact and have made this party to a crime merely an accessory. Under this crime, in order to be classified as an accessory, a person must furnish shelter, lodging, food and concealment, from another who has rightful custody.

Concealment under this act means more than mere silence. To harbor a person means to receive in a clandestine manner and without lawful authority a person for the purpose of concealment so that another having the right to lawful custody of such a person shall be deprived of the same. The "accessory" terminology may be used to describe the furnishing of shelter, lodging, or food in a clandestine manner or with concealment, and under certain circumstances, may be equally applicable to those acts divested of any accompanying secrecy.[19]

The third party to a crime in many states is called an accomplice. The word accomplice has a variety of meanings, and it is sometimes applied by the law to all who had a part in the commission of a crime, whatever their degree of complicity. Generally, however, the term is used to include only those who participate as principals and accessories before the fact. Thus, it usually excludes accessories after the fact. An accomplice can be defined as one who is liable to prosecution for the identical offense charged against a defendant (he is initially a principal). Any principal or conspirator, when called upon to testify in behalf of the state against his coconspirators, is identified as an accomplice.

The testimony of an accomplice is viewed with caution and therefore, evidence rules usually relate to the need for corroboration of the testimony of an accomplice. Usually, corroboration needs to be more than: 1) mere opportunity or motive, 2) failure of the defendant to testify, or 3) just to show the commission of an offense. However, corroboration can be sufficient if: 1) the defendant attempts flight and attempts to rig a false alibi, 2) if the defendant was apprehended in the possession of an instrument used in the commission of the crime, 3) if the defendant possesses stolen property from the scene, and 4) if the defendant confesses or admits guilt.

The testimony of an accomplice usually results in a reduction of the charges against him or in total immunity. Generally, the court has no objection in whole or in part for immunity after full and fair testimony. However, a miscarriage of justice may arise when an accomplice is granted immunity on a condition of testimony that is responsible for the conviction of coprincipals if this is the sole purpose of the testimony.

Endnotes

1. Perkins, Rollin, *Criminal Law and Procedure*, cases and materials (N.Y.: Foundation Press, 1972), p. 479.
2. *Tyre v. Settle*, 168, F. Supp. 7.
3. *Perkins on Criminal Law*, 2nd Ed. p. 859.
4. Ibid. pp. 859, 863.
5. Durham v. United States, 214 F. 2d 862.
6. People v. Henderson, 60 Cal 2nd, 482.
7. Bernard L. Diamond, *Sirhan B. Sirhan*, Psychology Today, (September 1969).
8. People v. Gorshen, 51 Cal 2nd, 716.
9. People v. Statley, 91 Cal App 2d Supp. 943.
10. People v. Zammuto, 117 N.E. 454.
11. People Ex rel. Hegeman vs. Corrigan, 87 N.E. 792.
12. State v. Vilfogle, 109 Conn. 124.
13. State v. Rutner, 66 Nevada, 127.
14. State v. Phillips, 80 West Virginia 748.
15. People v. Jones, 263 Illinois 564.
16. Avey v. State, 249 Maryland, 385.
17. People v. Ah Gee, 37 Cal App 1.
18. People v. Lengarnett, 129 Cal 364.
19. United States v. Grant, 55 F. 415.

QUESTIONS

1. Name five classes of individuals who are exempt from criminal liability.
2. What effect does age have upon criminal liability?
3. Name three tests of insanity and describe each.
4. What effect does diminished capacity have upon wrongful death situations?
5. On what occasions are married women and adults who are not insane exempt from criminal liability?
6. Define double jeopardy and state its effect upon the court process.
7. What effect does intoxication have upon specific intent statutes?
8. Define the three parties to a crime.
9. What differences exist between common law and modern law parties to a crime?
10. Give three examples each for principals, accessories, and accomplices.

Chapter Seven

AN OVERVIEW OF RELATED ENFORCEABLE LAWS

This chapter is included for the purpose of providing an opportunity to make application of the legal concepts previously studied. The material is an overview of the most commonly violated statutes and is not meant to give a complete orientation to substantive law. This section will be geared to enforceable law for purposes of comparison and uniformity. It is recommended that the student study each crime and point out the corpus delicti, type of intent, and any other legal concept which might be applicable.

CRIMES AGAINST PROPERTY AND PERSON

Theft

At common law theft or nonforcible appropriation of property was divided into three separate crimes; larceny, embezzlement, and obtaining title to property by false pretenses.

Larceny was defined as the trespassory taking and carrying away of personal property with intent to steal. The taking was trespassory in the sense that it was against the will of the owner or without his consent. If consent was given to the taking, and the consent was obtained by fraud, there was deemed a constructive trespass and the offense was referred to as larceny by trick.

The *mens-rea* element or mental condition necessary was the intent to steal the property at the time of taking. Any taking without such intent was not larceny. The requisite acts to constitute the crime were some form of an asportation or moving of the property in addition to a taking. This was generally considered satisfied if the property was severed from the possession or custody of the owner and moved in the slightest degree.

Embezzlement was the fraudulent conversion of personal property by a person to whom it was entrusted. In this crime, a party has been given possession of property by the owner. There is no trespassory taking and, therefore, embezzlement is not larceny. The party to whom the property has been entrusted later entertains the criminal scheme and appropriates the property for his own use. Here, the mens rea element is the intent to appropriate the property and utilize it for some purpose other than for that which the property was entrusted. The act necessary to establish embezzlement is the actual conversion of the property to some other use.

False Pretenses is defined as knowingly obtaining property of another by false representations of fact with intent to defraud. This crime is quite often confused with larceny by trick. In both crimes, property is given with consent, however such consent is obtained by fraud and thus in actuality there is a constructive trespass in both crimes. The difference being in the crime of false pretenses, property is obtained. This means that there was an intent by the owner to pass title and thus the wrongdoer "obtains" the property. In the crime of larceny by trick, mere possession is acquired by the wrongdoer. The owner consents to giving the wrongdoer possession of his property and does not intend to pass title to such property.

The *mens-rea* element in the crime of false pretenses consists of the intent to take title with full knowledge that the owner is laboring under untrue or false representations which prompt the passing of title. The acts required in this crime are the making of false promises or making untrue representations to the owner and subsequently taking possession of the property.

One method of resolving the problem of distinguishing the forms of theft is to consolidate them all into one general definition of theft. Thus, a consolidated theft section may now read: Every person who shall feloniously steal, take, carry, lead or drive away the personal property of another, or who shall fraudulently appropriate property which has been entrusted to him, or who shall knowingly and designedly, by any false or fraudulent representation or pretense, defraud any other person of money, labor, or real or personal property, or who causes or procures others to report falsely of his death or mercantile character and by thus imposing upon any person, obtains credit and thereby fraudulently gets or obtains possession of money or property or obtains the labor or service of another, is guilty of theft.[1]

Theft is usually divided into two degrees, grand

and petty. Grand theft is defined as theft of money, labor, or property exceeding $200.00 or some similar value, or the taking of property consisting of either an automobile, firearm, horse, mare, gelding, any bovine animal, any caprine animal, mule, jack, jenny, sheep, lamb, hog, sow, boar, gilt, barrow or pig. Petty theft includes all theft other than grand theft. The important difference is that petty theft is ordinarily a misdemeanor whereas grand theft may be punished as a felony.

Robbery

Robbery is considered a combination of assault and larceny. In essence, it is the forcible taking of property. At common law, as well as under present law, robbery is punished as a felony and is considered to be one of the most serious of all felonies.

The common law definition of robbery is codified or accepted by statute in most states. Robbery is the felonious taking of personal property in the possession of another, from his person or immediate presence, and against his will, accomplished by means of force or fear. The fear may be either of an unlawful injury to the person or property of the person robbed or any relative or family member. The fear may also be the fear of an immediate and unlawful injury to the person or property of anyone in the company of the person robbed at the time of the robbery.

At common law, different degrees of robbery were not recognized. However, two or more degrees of robbery are often provided for by statute. All robbery which is perpetrated by torture or by a person being armed with a dangerous or deadly weapon, and the robbery of any person who is performing his duties as operator of any motor vehicle, streetcar, or trackless trolley is robbery in the first degree. All other kinds of robbery are of the second degree. Although all robberies are punished as felonies, first degree robbery is punished more severely.

Extortion

The common-law crime of extortion was defined as the corrupt collection of an unauthorized or other unlawful fee by a public officer under color of his office. The concept of extortion has been expanded by statute, and the modern term for the crime is blackmail. Extortion is the obtaining of property from another, with his consent, or the obtaining of an official act of a public officer, induced by a wrongful use of force or fear, or under color of official right. This crime differs from robbery in that the property which is obtained is acquired with the victim's consent. However, since the acquisition has been induced through the wrongful use of force or fear, the conduct is criminal.

The fear which will constitute extortion varies somewhat from the fear induced in the crime of robbery. The fear may be induced by a threat, either—

1. To do an unlawful injury to the person or property of the individual threatened or of a third person; or,

2. To accuse the individual threatened, or any relative of his, or member of his family, of any crime; or
3. To expose, or to impute to him or them any deformity, disgrace or crime; or
4. To expose, any secret affecting him or them.

Burglary

At common law, burglary was essentially a crime against the habitation. The crime was the breaking and entering of a dwelling house in the nighttime with intent to commit a felony.

Again, modern statutes have expanded the common-law definition. Every person who enters any house, room, apartment, tenement, shop, warehouse, store, mill, barn, stable, outhouse, or other building, tent, vessel, railroad car, trailer coach, vehicle when the doors are locked, or aircraft, with intent to commit grand or petty larceny or any felony is guilty of burglary. The common law requirements of a "breaking," a "dwelling house" and "in the nighttime" have usually been abandoned. Burglary, by statute, has also been divided into degrees, whereas at common law there was only one substantive crime of burglary. The most serious degree of burglary includes burglary of an inhabited dwelling house, trailer coach, or building, in the nighttime, or burglary in the daytime, while armed with a deadly weapon. All other types of burglary are of the second degree. The differences in degree are important in that burglary of the first degree is subject to more severe punishment.

Burglary is a specific intent crime. The *mens-rea* element is met only when the actor enters a structure or vehicle with the intent to commit either petty or grand larceny or any felony. If he entertains the intent after entry, the crime of burglary is not complete. The *actus reus* or act necessary to constitute statutory burglary is the mere entry into a structure or entry into a locked car. At common law, the act required an actual breaking of the structure.

Arson

Arson, at common law, was the malicious burning of a dwelling house of another. The requirement that the burned structure be a dwelling house was essential to establishment of the crime. The crime has again undergone expansion by statute. Arson is now defined as the malicious burning of any trailer, coach, dwelling house, or any kitchen, shop, barn, stable, or other outhouse. There are generally no degrees of arson, and any such act of burning is treated as a felony. Arson is also a specific intent crime. The actor must entertain a malicious state of mind. He must intentionally set the fire, or his conduct must be extremely reckless, the obvious risk that a fire will result. The act necessary is the setting of the fire or placing in motion some force which produces the fire.

Forgery

The common-law and the modern statutory definition of forgery is essentially the same. Forgery is the making of a false instrument or the material alteration of an existing instrument, where such instrument has apparent legal significance, with the intent to defraud. The instruments or writings that have such apparent legal significance are listed in the forgery statutes. They include bonds, promissory notes, deeds, leases, indentures, wills, certificates of stock, and so on.

The basic crime of forgery requires three elements: a writing or other subject of forgery, false making or alteration, and an intent to defraud. The second element constitutes the *actus reus* while the third element is the *mens-rea* requirement of the crime.

Assault and Battery

Battery is a willful and unlawful use of force or violence upon the person of another. It requires a touching but does not necessarily result in an injury. An assault is an unlawful attempt to commit a battery and, thus, may occur without a battery. The common-law concept is the same as the modern statutory crime. A simple assault or battery is a misdemeanor and is characterized as a general intent crime. No specific intent is required. The intentional doing of the act or criminal negligence in causing the harm or attempted harm is sufficient to satisfy the *mens-rea* requirement.

Aggravated assaults or batteries are treated as felonies, for example, assault with a deadly weapon or with means likely to produce great bodily harm. Most aggravated crimes require a specific intent and a general criminal intent is not sufficient. These include assault with intent to commit enumerated felonies and the most common of these crimes are assault with intent to murder, assault with intent to rape, or assault with caustic chemicals. Here a specific designated state of mind must be proven on the part of the suspect.

False Imprisonment

By statute and at common law, false imprisonment is the unlawful violation of the personal liberty of another. The crux of this crime is a confinement or detention without sufficient legal authority. Ordinarily, the crime is punishable as a misdemeanor. However, if the confinement is achieved by use of violence, menace, fraud, or deceit, it is punishable as a felony. This crime is a general intent crime in that there need not exist any specific intent to unlawfully or unreasonably confine. The intent to confine or intentionally commit the act that causes confinement is all that is necessary.

Mayhem

A person who unlawfully and maliciously deprives a human being of a member of his body, or disables, disfigures, or renders it useless, or cuts or disables the tongue, or puts out an eye, or slits the nose, ear, or lip is guilty of mayhem. The statutory law has undergone substantial change from the common-law concept of mayhem which was the malicious deprivation of a member, in fighting, rendering one less able, either to defend himself or to annoy his adversary.

The crime of mayhem was a felony at common law as well as today. Mayhem has also retained a specific intent requirement. The defendant's conduct must be malicious. As defined earlier, this is satisfied where the defendant has intended to disfigure or disable, or, where due to his reckless conduct there was an obvious indifference to the likelihood of a disfigurement resulting from his acts.

Rape

Rape is an act of sexual intercourse, accomplished with a female not the wife of the perpetrator, under either of the following circumstances.

1. Where she is incapable, through lunacy or other unsoundness of mind, whether temporary or permanent, of giving legal consent;
2. Where she resists, but her resistance is overcome by force or violence;
3. Where she is prevented from resisting by threats of great and immediate bodily harm, accompanied by apparent power of execution or by any intoxicating substance administered;
4. Where she is at the time unconscious of the nature of the act, and this is known to the accused;

5. Where she submits under the belief that the person committing the act is her husband, and this belief is induced by an artifice, pretense, or concealment practiced by the accused, with intent to induce such belief.

Rape as defined, was also recognized at common law. However, under many statutes, there is in addition to the above offense what is popularly known as statutory rape. This offense consists of unlawful sexual intercourse accomplished with a female not the wife of the perpetrator, where the female is under the age of eighteen years. No such offense existed at common law.

The statutory age varies from state to state, ranging from ten to twenty-one years of age. If the perpetrator has reasonable cause to believe that the woman is of age, he can not be convicted. The *mens-rea* element in this crime, as well as in the regular rape situation, requires no specific intent to commit the crime. Intent to have sexual relations or criminal negligence is sufficient to constitute the crime. The act of statutory rape, as well as in other cases, is the sexual penetration of the female.

Kidnaping

At common law, kidnaping was defined as the forcible abduction or stealing away of a person from his own country and carrying him into another. This definition or concept of kidnaping has since become obsolete. Kidnaping, by statute, is the forcible or fraudulent stealing or abduction of another person.

Simple kidnaping is a general intent crime and there need not be a specific intent to do a particular act. The acts necessary to constitute the crime encompass a forcible restraint and asportation of the victim. However, kidnaping for ransom, extortion, or robbery require a specific designated state of mind.

Homicide

Homicide is defined as the killing of a human being by another. Under statute, homicide includes first degree murder, second degree murder, voluntary and involuntary manslaughter. In situations where a homicide is justifiable or excusable, it is innocent homicide and therefore not punishable as a crime.

Before a defendant may be charged with any form of homicide, whether it be murder or manslaughter, the defendant's acts must be the actual and proximate cause of death. The rules regarding causation would therefore be applied. Also, the death must occur within one year and a day or some similar limited period after which the defendant's act or such acts are not deemed to be the cause of death.

Murder is the unlawful killing of a human being, or a fetus, with malice aforethought. This is a specific intent crime in that the *mens-rea* requirement needed is malice aforethought. Malice aforethought is a man-endangering state of mind where no circumstances of justification, mitigation, or excuse exists. If such a state of mind exists and the defendant kills another, the conduct may be either first or second degree murder.

First degree murder is that which is perpetrated

by means of poison, or lying in wait, torture, bombing, or by any other kind of willful, deliberate, and premeditated killing. All other kinds of murders are of the second degree.

Manslaughter is the unlawful killing of a human being without malice. It may be voluntary, involuntary, or vehicular. Manslaughter is voluntary when one kills in a sudden quarrel or heat of passion. It is involuntary when death results from the commission of an act without due regard or caution. When malice cannot be established pursuant to a culpable homicide, manslaughter may be charged. Manslaughter does not require a specific intent or *mens rea.* It is a general intent crime and hence may be sustained in circumstances which are insufficient to establish murder.

Vehicular manslaughter remains a felony when gross negligence is present and is classified as a misdemeanor when death occurs without the existence of gross negligence.

Child Molesting

Statutes define a child molester as any person who willfully and lewdly commits any lewd act on any part of the body of a child with the intent of arousing the passions of either party. The words willfully and lewdly identify this act as a specific intent crime. It is not necessary that the passions of either party actually become aroused, only that there be a touching with the intent of arousal. Consent is immaterial. Generally the child must be under a specified age, usually under fourteen years old.

CRIMES AGAINST PUBLIC DECENCY, MORALITY, AND THE PUBLIC PEACE

Adultery and Fornication

Adultery and fornication were punished by the Church as ecclesiastical offenses, but were not recognized as common-law crimes. It was felt that certain types of misconduct should be subject exclusively to the jurisdiction of the Church. Adultery violated the marriage vow and was, therefore, a punishable offense. Adultery was sexual intercourse with one other than a spouse. Fornication was the act of intercourse while unmarried. In modern times these offenses are made crimes by statute in some states. Adultery is an offense in only slightly more half of the fifty states and fornication in about only one-third. There seems to be a deep-seated and widely held opinion to the effect that this is an area which should be left to religious, educational, or other social influences. (Perkins on Criminal Law 2nd Ed. 379).

In most states, illicit intercourse by an unmarried person (fornication), is not punishable by statute. However, if a married person has relations with a third person, married or unmarried, the defendant may be guilty of adultery, a misdemeanor. Such statutes have sometimes been interpreted to mean that cohabitation as well as sexual relations are necessary to constitute the crime; in other words some additional proof that the man & woman have lived together is necessary.

Bigamy

Bigamy can be considered the status of a person who has more than one spouse at the same time. At common law this offense was also an ecclesiastical crime. Bigamy was considered a direct attack upon the existence of the marriage relationship, and hence the offenders were dealt with harshly. Even under most modern statutes, bigamy is punishable as a felony.

Bigamy is defined as having a husband or wife living while married to another person. Bigamy may be punished as a felony calling for possible imprisonment of ten years or by a fine. However, a belief in good faith that one is free to marry is a defense to bigamy.

Incest

Incest is either marriage or sexual intercourse without marriage between persons who are too closely related in degrees of consanguinity. It was not an offense under the common law, but was only punishable as an ecclesiastical offense. Such acts were viewed as offenses against morality and were dealt with harshly. The same views persist today, and the acts constituting incest are by statute made felonies in all states.

Parties within a close degree of consanguinity or blood relatives including stepfathers and stepmothers are guilty of incest if they marry, commit fornication, or commit adultery. Consent by both parties is not a defense, society viewing such acts with contempt regardless of the circumstances. Accordingly, incest is punishable as a felony with a possible 50 year prison sentence.

Seduction

There was no crime known as seduction at common law, however, such an offense is generally provided for by statute. A male can be charged with seduction when, under promise of marriage, he seduces and has sexual intercourse with an unmarried female of previous chaste character. This offense is punishable as a felony under many state statutes. However, it must be shown that the promise of marriage was the inducing factor in procurring the woman's surrender. Also, for the woman to be of chaste character means that she was *virgo intacta*, or a virgin.

Obscenity

Obscenity statutes are common in the United States, with practically every state having some for regulation and prohibition. The statutes cover pornographic literature, plays, live sexual shows, and moving pictures or films. Federal regulation is also involved. It is a federal offense to mail or advertise by mail any obscene material. (18 U.S.C.A. sect. 1461). Some cities and counties have imposed local ordinances to deal with such conduct. Legislatures have attempted to confront the problem by providing for criminal treatment of every person who knowingly sends, brings into the state, or in the state prepares or prints obscene material with intent to distribute or to exhibit it. However, the real difficulty presents itself in determining what is or is not obscene matter. Obscene matter is usually defined by statutes based on Supreme Court decisions, such as any matter taken as a whole, the predominant appeal of which to the average person, applying contemporary standards, is to prurient interests and is matter which taken as a whole is utterly without redeeming social importance. The recent case of *Miller v. California*, (1973) 93 S. Ct. 2607, lays down new guide lines as to what obscenity is, and how it should be defined. The Supreme Court stated that the matter or work taken as a whole, must have serious literary, artistic, political, or scientific value and it renounces the utterly-without-redeeming-social-value test which has been applied in California. The court further stressed that contemporary community standards by which such matter is viewed need not be the national standard. This raises the question as to whether each city, town, county, or state may impose its individual standard and deal with obscenity accordingly. The full effect of the Miller case upon national obscenity laws has not yet been determined.

Most objections to obscenity laws have been based on constitutional grounds in that such regulation amounts to censorship and violation of freedom of speech and the press. However, it has been continually held that obscenity is not protected by the constitution and obscenity is not within the area of constitutionally protected freedom of speech or press. The salient issue is the determination of whether a particular matter is obscene. If it is not, then constitutional guarantees attach thereto.

Other Crimes Against Decency and Morals

Numerous other forms of conduct are characterized as crimes and sometimes are punished rather severely. Such crimes include sodomy, buggery, fellatio, cunnilingus, and sexual perversion. Other crimes which are punished, generally as misdemeanors, include prostitution, pimping, indecent exposure, and nonsupport of children.

Breach of the Peace and Related Offenses

Breach of peace is defined as maliciously and willfully disturbing the peace or quiet of any neighborhood or person, by loud or unusual noise or offensive conduct or threatening, traducing, quarreling, challenging to fight, or fighting. The broad language of statutes regarding disturbing the peace, like the one quoted above, sometimes inspires prosecutions for conduct which is in no sense criminal. It is not uncommon for convictions to be overturned on grounds that such conviction has violated the defendant's rights to due process of law as guaranteed by the Fourteenth Amendment. The words "maliciously" and "willfully" identify breech of the peace as a specific intent section. The United States Supreme Court has indicated that this crime applies to actions made by the defendant, not words which could be constitutionally protected by the First Amendment. *Cohen* v. *California* (1971) 403 U.S. 15. In order for this statute to be applied legally, the California Supreme Court interprets the section as requiring that a prohibited act incite or threaten to incite others to violence.

Other types of conduct which are commonly made crimes and are considered disturbances of public tranquility including an affray, dueling, illegal prize fighting, unlawful assembly, rout, riot, lynching, disturbance of assembly, and forcible entry and detainer.

Disorderly Conduct

This crime under many state statutes encompasses various different types of conduct. Every person who commits any of the following acts could be guilty of disorderly conduct.

1. Soliciting in public or engages in lewd or dissolute conduct
2. Soliciting or engaging in prostitution
3. Loitering, begging, trespassing
4. Public intoxication
5. Molesting or loitering near children
6. Peeking into doors or windows of any inhabited building upon the private property of another.

These types of laws have been under critical examination in recent years. The United States Supreme Court has pointed out that the application of loitering and disorderly conduct statutes must be consistent with due process.

Related Enforceable Codes

I. Some states regulate narcotics by way of penal code statutes and others set up a separate code or regulate narcotics through health and safety measures or through pharmacy-type drug statutes. Wherever such statutes are found, the following crimes are most commonly described:

1. Simple possession of prohibited drugs, narcotics or marijuana in small quantities for personal use.
2. Possession of larger quantities for purposes of sale.
3. Actual sales or transportation of any quantity of prohibited drugs, narcotics, or marijuana. *Sales to minors are treated as most serious.*
4. Possession of contrivances and equipment used to assist in the consumption of drugs, narcotics, and marijuana.

II. States regulate business activities and the professions through enforcement of qualifications to obtain licenses and by revocation or suspension of licenses when a licensee has done a prohibited act. For example, lawyers can be disbarred for committing an act which involves moral turpitude or for misrepresenting facts to a court. A doctor will also lose his license for similar unprofessional acts.

III. Criminal punishment may be imposed for violation of city or county ordinances, such as discharging a firearm or hunting in prohibited areas, illegal parking, traffic regulation, curfew, zoning requirement violations, and so on. These local agencies can act only in areas where the state has not already acted or else with specific state permission. Clearly these violations are all misdemeanors.

IV. The United States Code codifies the general, permanent laws of the United States. Though these various federal laws specify many crimes, it must be remembered that there is federal jurisdiction only when certain factors are involved: interstate commerce, officers, or property of the United States, or other acts affecting agencies of the United States. The most common federal crimes would probably be smuggling of narcotics across a border, federal bank robbery, counterfeiting, and income tax evasion. All federal cases, of course, must be tried in federal courts.

Endnote

1. California Penal Code, sec. 484.

QUESTIONS

1. Define and distinguish between the four types of theft.
2. What is the chief difference between robbery and theft?

3. Under what conditions does the crime of robbery become first degree?
4. Define the different types of fear which constitute extortion.
5. List the corpus delicti of burglary and distinguish between first and second degree burglary.
6. What primary differences exist between simple assault and battery and aggravated assault and battery?
7. What are the five different types of legal rape?
8. What are the basic differences between murder and manslaughter?
9. What legal manifestations must be present before a piece of literature can be deemed obscene.
10. Analyze the case decisions Cohen and Bushman as they effect the crime, breech of the peace.
11. Name six different types of disorderly conduct.

Appendix

AN OVERVIEW OF CONSTITUTIONAL GUARANTEES

Constitutional rights to fair and orderly procedures for asserting governmental power against defendants.

A. *Preliminary Note. Application of Bill of Rights to States—the Doctrine of Incorporation*

1. The famous case of *Barron* v. *Baltimore* (U.S. Sup.Ct., 1833) established that the first eight Amendments of the Constitution (the Bill of Rights) were applicable only to action by the federal government.

2. In recent years, under the leadership of Justice Black, a powerful minority of the U.S Sup. Ct., which included Justices Murphy, Rutledge and Douglas, has pressed for an adoption of the view that the Fourteenth Amendment effected an incorporation of the first eight Amendments, so that the first eight Amendments would be applicable to the states.

3. The majority of the Court has refused to accept the "incorporation theory", and has instead relied upon a more flexible and indefinite concept: That "due process" provides assurance that the states will be required to adhere to those minimum procedural and substantive rights which are *implicit in the concept of ordered liberty* (Cardozo, J. in *Palko* v. *Connecticut*, USSCt.1937) and do not offend "Traditional notions of fair play and substantial justice" (Stone, J. in *International Shoe Co.* v. *Washington*, USSCt.1945).

4. THUS TODAY *many* of the specific rights mentioned in the first eight Amendments are regarded as incorporated in the Fourteenth Amendment, but *some* are not. This is sometimes referred to as *selective incorporation.* In practical effect, this means that each case must be evaluated upon its own facts where state action is involved; and that stricter standards of constitutionality may be applied to federal proceedings (in light of the express limitations of the Bill of Rights) than to state proceedings (where the more flexible concept of "due process" is the test).

5. NOTE ALSO THAT DUE PROCESS HAS ITS OWN INDEPENDENT MEANING, and imposes limits on *both* state and federal proceedings *in addition to* those restrictions which are spelled out in the Bill of Rights. (See below)

B. *Preliminary Note: Significance of Equal Protection Clause as a Safeguard of Procedural Fairness for Criminal Defendants*

1. *Jury trials:* it has long been held that trial before a jury which has been selected by a system

that deliberately and systematically excludes qualified classes of the citizenry from jury service for arbitrary reasons (such as race and color) violates the Equal Protection Clause as well as Due Process. The burden of showing that the system is in fact a nondiscriminatory one shifts to the state after the defendant has presented a prima facie case by showing that a designated class of citizens (e.g., Negroes) has not been represented on any juries for a substantial period of time. *Hernandez* v. *Texas*, USSCt.1954:

a. NOTE: the defendant is not entitled to have any members of his own race actually on the jury that tries him, as long as the selection system is fairly set up.
b. *Exclusion of women* from jury service: the practice in some states of excluding women from jury service has not yet been reviewed by the Supreme Court in any modern case. However, the Florida practice of limiting women jurors to those who had voluntarily registered for jury duty, although all men were subject to such duty without registering for it, was held valid. This distinction between men and women is not arbitrary or irrational, in light of the importance of women in the home as mothers and homemakers. The issue whether it would be constitutional to exclude women altogether was left open for consideration at a later time. *Hoyt* v. *Florida*, USSCt.1961 (affirming conviction of woman for murdering her husband by all-male jury).
c. *Sufficiency of evidence of racial discrimination:* A mere conflict of evidence on issue of racial discrimination in jury selection is *not* enough to sustain a holding of validity of a challenged selection system. The state must convince the Supreme Court—which independently evaluates the evi-

dence and is not bound by the lower court's decision—that there is a convincing and reasonable explanation for prima facie disparity between population ratio and jury membership ratio of races. *Coleman* v. *Alabama* (1967); *Jones* v. *Georgia* (1967).

2. *Grand Juries:* a discriminatory system for selecting the grand jury, which systematically excludes Negroes from membership, violates Equal Protection—and even though the trial is before a properly selected jury, and is in all ways fair, the fact that the defendant was *indicted* by the discriminatorily selected grand jury requires that the *conviction be reversed.* Reason: this is the only effective way to induce states to desist from discriminatory selection of grand juries, whose function is to protect citizens against unfounded prosecutions as well as to indict those believed guilty. *Cassell* v. *Texas*, USSCt.1950.

3. *Equal justice for indigents:*

a. The indigent defendant who desires to take an appeal from a criminal conviction, where a transcript of the evidence is necessary to present the issues on appeal, is entitled to have a transcript provided for him at the expense of the State. Otherwise his inability to prosecute an effective appeal, due to his poverty, would result in an invidious discrimination, since the wealthy defendant could prosecute an appeal by paying for his transcript. The indigent is entitled to the same quality of justice as the wealthy litigant. *Griffin* v. *Illinois*, USSCt.1956.

b. Under California practice, an indigent appellant could obtain free assistance of counsel on his appeal only after the appellate court investigated the record and determined that counsel might be of aid to the court and appellant. *Held*: Denial of Equal Protection. Rich appellant may hire counsel and get benefit of advocate seeking for defects in judgement. Indigent is deprived of this advantage by reason of his poverty; and court's determination whether to appoint counsel or not is not an adequate substitute, for court acts impartially, unaided by searching and probing of an advocate which may turn up points overlooked by the court. Hence, court must appoint an attorney for any indigent appellant. *Douglas* v. *California*, USSCt.1963.

c. Full extent of the Equal Protection doctrine, as ensuring the indigent defendant "equal justice" to the wealthy defendant, is still emerging, and is presently uncertain. For example, must trial court provide funds with which appointed counsel for indigent defendant may make an adequate fact investigation in support of a defense? With which to hire expert witnesses? Etc.

d. Other illustrations of the *Griffin* doctrine in recent cases include:

- refusal of trial court to entertain habeas corpus petition because of inability of indigent petitioner to pay filing fee, held unconstitutional: *Smith* v. *Bennett*, USSCt.1961.
- state law giving indigent appellants a free transcript only if public defender approved, held unconstitutional, since wealthy defendant could obtain a transcript without such prior approval: *Lane* v. *Brown*, USSCt.1963.
- state rule which permitted indigent appellant to have free transcript only when trial judge

certified the errors claimed were not frivolous, held unconstitutional, for wealthy appellant was under no such burden: *Draper* v. *Washington*, USSCt.1963.

- indigent convict who seeks to review denial of habeas corpus petition by filing new petition in appellate court held automatically entitled to free transcript of evidentiary hearing in trial court to assist in obtaining meaningful review, where wealthy defendant could buy one: *Gardner* v. *California* (1969).
- indigent convicted of misdemeanor drunk driving held entitled to free transcript to perfect appeal; *Griffin* doctrine is not limited to felony convictions. *Williams* v. *Oklahoma City* (1969).

C. *Constitutional protections granted to persons accused of crime.*

Preliminary Note: The range of constitutional provisions that should be considered in cases involving criminal defense rights can be remembered by the following mnemonic device: "*J*ustice for *C*riminals *S*urely *D*emands *I*mproved *I*ncentive *P*ay to *C*reate *B*etter *C*ity *P*olice *D*epartments" Each of the underlined introductory letters in the foregoing sentence is the key to each of the twelve topics which follow:

1. *Jury Trial Right:*

a. *In federal cases*, the Sixth Amendment requires a twelve person jury, with unanimous verdict, unless waived by the defendant. Waiver, however, is not effective unless made knowingly and voluntarily and fully shown in the record. (Silence of the record will not be presumed to support a waiver.) This right obtains in all felony cases and (apparently) in all other cases which are *more* than mere "petty" offenses—i.e., offenses punishable by *more* than six months in jail or $500 fine or both. Offenses punishable by less severe sentences may be tried without a jury. *Frank* v. United States (1969) (jury trial held not required in contempt of court case, where punishment was suspended sentence and three years probation, i.e., neither fine nor jail sentence.)

The Sixth Amendment right of jury trial applies in contempt of court proceedings as well as other criminal prosecutions. *Bloom* v. *Illinois* (1968) (overruling prior cases to contrary).

b. *In state cases*, the Fourteenth Amendment requires a jury trial in all serious criminal prosecutions (other than petty offenses), unless the defendant waives his rights knowingly, voluntarily, and on the record. The jury trial right is a fundamental one, designed to protect against governmental tyranny and oppression by over zealous prosecutors or biased judges. Hence, is incorporated in Due Process. *Duncan* v. *Louisiana* (1968); *Bloom* v. *Illinois* (1968).

NOTE WELL: Two important issues were left unresolved by these decisions: (1) *What is a "Petty" offense?* The Court suggests that the upper limit may be one year's imprisonment, but it may also be six months (consistent with the federal rule of practice). In addition, there may be offenses for which light punishment is prescribed but which, because of other collateral consequences (e.g., danger of government oppression; special need for jury consensus in resolving issues for which judges have no special competence, etc.) may be deemed "serious". Best approach: weigh all circumstances from a practical viewpoint. 2) *Must states give a jury trial according to federal standards?* Many states provide for less-than-twelve men on jury, or for less than a unanimous vote. How about standards governing the degree of a judge's control of jury deliberations (e.g., right of judge to comment on evidence)? How about the practice of selecting jurors by voir dire examination, challenges, grounds for challenge, etc.? The court did not resolve these problems. Fortas, J., who concurred in the majority opinion, expressly stated (in a special concurring opinion) that he would not require federal standards to be observed by the states as long as the essence of a jury trial was given the criminal defendant. Best approach: evaluate the practical importance of the practice in light of the facts.

c. *Death qualified jury:* The jury must be a fair-minded one that is reasonably representative of the community's sense of values relevant to criminal justice. Hence, in a capital case, Due Process forbids the exclusion of jurors merely because they have conscientious scruples against, or moral opposition to, the death sentence. Since substantial numbers of people have such views, their exclusion from jury service would mean that the defendant would be tried by a jury that could not rationally express "the conscience of the community on the ultimate question of life and death," but which had been selected and organized to return the death sentence. *Witherspoon* v. *Illinois* (1968).

NOTE IMPLICATIONS: The *Witherspoon* rule applies only where the jury has discretion to decide the sentence—whether to impose imprisonment or a death sentence. The determination of *guilt* was held valid, since the exclusion of persons opposed to capital punishment did not substantially increase the risk of erroneous conviction of guilt of the crime charged. *Accord: Bumper* v. *North Carolina* (1958).

The rule only forbids exclusion of prospective jurors who have *general* objections to capital punishment. It is still permissible to exclude from the jury persons who express a fixed and unchangeable position—who state unequivocally that they would *never* vote for a death sentence no matter what the evidence showed. *Boulden* v. *Holman* (1969).

d. *Waiver of jury trial right:* The right to a jury trial may be waived by the defendant, but waiver will be constitutionally acceptable only if the record affirmatively shows that there was no coercion, inducement or threat, and that the waiver was made voluntarily by the defendant with an understanding of its consequences.

Example: Plea of guilty *held* constitutionally impermissible basis for conviction, where record failed to demonstrate that it was given knowingly and voluntarily. Trial judge has a duty to explore these matters, and make a record on them, before he accepts a plea of guilty; for such a plea, in effect, amounts to a waiver of right to jury trial, as well as waiver of privilege against self-incrimination and waiver of right to confront and cross-examine accusers. Courts cannot assume waiver of such important rights from a silent record. *Boykin* v. *Alabama* (1969).

Example: Lindberg Kidnapping Law *held* unconstitutional insofar as it authorizes a death penalty only when recommended by a jury, since the risk of a death sentence tends to induce defendant to waive a jury trial (or plead guilty) involuntarily. *United States* v. *Jackson* (1968).

2. *Right to Counsel for Criminal Defendant:*

a. *In federal cases*, the Sixth Amendment provides a right to counsel, including appointed counsel for indigents, in all serious criminal proceedings. The right may be waived—if waiver is intelligent and voluntary—but the facts supporting a valid waiver must appear affirmatively in the record.
b. *In state cases*, Due Process requires the same right of counsel to be assured as in federal cases, including appointed counsel for indigent defendants. *Gideon* v. *Wainwright* (1963). As in the federal cases, a knowing and intelligent waiver, if demonstrated affirmatively in the record, is acceptable; but the state has the burden of showing that such a waiver in fact occurred, and it will not be presumed from a silent record. *Carnley* v. *Cochran* (1962).
c. *Scope of right to counsel:* The criminal defendant has a right to advice and advocacy by counsel at any stage of a criminal proceeding at which the services of an attorney could conceivably assist materially in protecting the rights of the defendant. Thus, it extends to pre-trial as well as post-trial proceedings, and is not limited to the trial itself.

Example: Preliminary hearing on criminal charge is a critical stage of proceedings against defendant; hence a plea of guilty given at this point, when defendant was unrepresented by counsel, is vitiated by denial of Due Process and cannot be employed to cross-examine defendant (for impeachment purposes) in trial on a different charge arising out of same general circumstances. *Arsenault* v. *Massachusetts* (1968).

Example: Indigent defendant is entitled to counsel on appeal from criminal conviction, who will serve to advance interests of appellant as an *advocate* and not as an amicus curiae. Thus, defendant is denied effective right of counsel if attorney assigned on appeal merely reports to the court that he regards the appeal as without merit, and requests that he be relieved of further responsibility. If in fact, counsel believes the appeal to be "wholly frivolous' or utterly without any arguable points, he may ask leave to withdraw; but in so doing, he must brief all possibly arguable points for the court, and advise why he regards them as completely without merit. In this way, the indigent defendant will secure substantially the same level of advocacy as the wealthy defendant, as required by Due Process and Equal Protection. *Anders* v. *Calif.* (1967).

Example: Denial of counsel at proceeding to revoke probation violates Due Process, since counsel could assist defendant materially by (a) persuading court to be lenient in sentence to be served if probation is revoked; (b) establishing circumstances to cast doubt on reliability of grounds asserted for proposed revocation of probation; (c) showing the violation of terms of probation was relatively trivial, not warranting revocation but some lesser sanction instead; and

(d) making an adequate record for purposes of appeal from revocation order. *Mempa* v. *Rhay* (1967).

Note Implications: The *Mempa* rule suggests that right to counsel may be constitutionally required at all sentencing proceedings. *Unanswered issues include:* Is a prisoner entitled to counsel at a parole board hearing to determine whether he should be paroled? At a hearing to revoke parole of a prisoner? [Note that parole is traditionally distinguished from probation; parole is a way of serving a prison sentence "outside the prison walls" while probation is regarded as supervisory treatment in lieu of a prison sentence.] At a hearing before Adult Authority to determine length of custody under indeterminate sentence law? At clemency hearing before Governor?

d. *Interrogation of suspects: Miranda Doctrine:* The Supreme Court has noted that the privilege against self-incrimination can be effectively preserved only if the suspect is aware of his rights. In order to safeguard this privilege, the prosecution is forbidden to use in evidence any statements of the accused made during custodial interrogation (i.e, after the person has been taken into custody or deprived of his freedom of action in a significant way) unless the following, or other equally effective procedural steps are taken: the person must be warned that (1) he has a right to remain silent, (2) any statement he makes may be used in evidence against him, (3) he has a right to consult counsel and have an attorney present during the interrogation, and (4) if he is indigent, an attorney will be provided for him without charge. Moreover, the person being questioned may at any time, even though he has already answered some questions, decline to answer any further, or decline to answer until he has consulted an attorney. Only if the statements of the accused are made after a voluntary, intelligent and knowing waiver—which must be proven by the prosecution, and *mere silence or lack of protest is not enough to show such a deliberate and knowing waiver*—can the statements be introduced in evidence. *Miranda* v. *Arizona; Vignera* v. *New York; Westover* v. *United States; California* v. *Stewart*, June 1966. (5-4 vote.)

Note: In these cases, the Court also pointed out certain important corollary rules: a) The four-point warning must always be given, and the courts will not inquire into such matters as the defendant's age, intelligence, knowledge of constitutional rights, etc. to excuse non-compliance with the warning rules. b) No distinction can be drawn between direct confessions and incriminating admissions which fall short of confessions; nor can any different rule apply to merely "exculpatory" statements of an accused. These rules will be applied to *any* statement of the accused made during custodial interrogation. c) The states are free to devise other methods for giving full protection to the right of silence, but such methods must be at least as effective as those required by the *Miranda* rules above.

Subsequent decisions have also held that *Miranda* rules are *not* limited to questioning of suspects at the police station. They also apply when a suspect is questioned in jail, where he is being held in custody on an unrelated charge or under an unrelated conviction. *Mathis* v. *United States* (1968) (Miranda held applicable to "routine" tax investigation questioning of taxpayer in state prison). Likewise, they must be complied with when the suspect is being questioned in his own home or on a public street, if he is not free to leave. *Orozco* v. *Texas* (1969).

3. *Search and Seizure: Freedom from Unreasonable Violation of Privacy*

a. In *federal* cases, the Fourth Amendment is regarded as not only preventing unlawful searches and seizures, but also requires evidence so seized to be ruled inadmissible. (*Weeks* v. *United States*, U.S. Sup.Ct., 1914).

b. In *state* cases, the Search and Seizure provision is deemed incorporated into Due Process, and requires exclusion of illegally seized evidence from state trial under same rules and standards as required by Fourth Amendment in federal prosecutions. *Mapp* v. *Ohio*, USSCt.1961.

   - *Oral fruits of illegal search:* if the defendant, in the course of an illegal search, makes oral statements which constitute incrimination, or which implicate others or lead to discovery of incriminating evidence, all such oral statements and their fruits must be excluded under the exclusionary rule, as well as physical evidence discovered in the illegal search. Otherwise, the protective purposes of the exclusionary rule would be frustrated. *Wong Sun* v. *United States*, USSCt. 1963.
   - In the course of a *valid* search, the police may seize *any* evidence properly discovered by them, and are not limited (as certain lower courts occasionally ruled) to contraband, wea-

pons, instruments of crime, or the fruits of crime. The fact that the things seized are "mere evidence" is immaterial, as is the fact that the search produced evidence of a *different* crime than that which justified the search. *Warden* v. *Hayden* (1967).

- Failure to object to admission of illegally seized evidence may amount to waiver of 4th Amendment rights, if done knowingly and with defendant's understanding of possible consequences. *Henry* v. *Mississippi* (1965).
- An objection to admissibility of illegally seized evidence can only be made by the person whose right of privacy was violated in connection with the seizure. Thus, for example, evidence illegally seized from A (e.g., conversations illegally overheard on a "bug") may not be excluded on objection by B, unless B's rights were also violated. BUT the owner of a house illegally "bugged" could object to any evidence so seized, since his rights as owner were violated as to all. *Alderman* v. *United States* (1969).

c. *Nature of the right: interest in privacy.* The essence of the Fourth Amendment right against unreasonable searches and seizures is protection against arbitrary invasions of personal *privacy* by public officials. Cases which formerly appeared to treat the right as primarily aimed at preventing physical intrusions upon private *property* have been overruled on this point. *Katz* v. *United States* (1967).

Example: Warrantless search of union records, in office of union official, and resulting seizure of union records that tended to incriminate the official, *HELD* violation of 4th Amendment. The fact that the premises were not owned by the defendant official, and that the seized records were those of the union and not of the defendant, makes no difference. The union office was a quasi-private place where the defendant had a right to privacy secured against unconstitutional intrusions by the police. *Mancusi* v. *DeForte* (1968).

Example: Fingerprint evidence taken from defendant who was taken into custody and questioned, along with numerous others during a "dragnet" type investigation of a reported rape, *HELD* inadmissible, where taken during the arrest and detention which was not supported by probable cause or by an arrest warrant. 4th Amendment protects against unreasonable seizure of the *person* as well as of property, and evidence taken from the person under these circumstances thus violates 4th Amendment policy to safeguard against intrusion of personal privacy by "dragnet" types of investigatory arrests. *Davis* v. *Mississippi* (1969).

d. *Example: Electronic surveillance* (e.g., wiretaps, bugging, etc.) comes within the purview of the 4th Amendment, since it constitutes an intrusion upon privacy of communications, together with the "seizure" of spoken words. Thus, the results of such surveillance are admissible in evidence only if made under 4th Amendment standards, which generally requires the prior approval of an independent magistrate upon an adequate showing of probably cause. *Berger* v. *New York* (1967); *Katz* v. *United States* (1967).

NOTE: Because of the special circumstances involving electronic surveillance, the Court has indicated that special safeguards may be required in the form of court authorizations to "bug" private conversations: the authorization must be based on probable cause to believe that incriminating statements will be overheard, and should limit the eavesdropping to particular conversations or to designated times and places, over a designated period of days, subject to periodic reporting to the judge as to results achieved or other appropriate limitations designed to prevent wholesale and indiscriminate intrusions into personal privacy.

Note Also: Since the "fruits" of an illegal seizure are inadmissible, a defendant who learns that he has been under illegal electronic surveillance (even though none of the evidence so developed was introduced at his trial) is entitled to inspect *all* of the records of that surveillance in order to lay the basis for proof that *other* evidence, which *was* used against him at the trial, was discovered as a result of the illegal search (i.e., was the "fruit of the poisonous tree") and was thus inadmissible. *Alderman* v. *United States* (1969).

e. *Search warrants and warrant standards:* Ordinarily, a search of private property for incriminating evidence must be supported by a search warrant issued by a magistrate on a showing of probable cause. If the warrant itself is illegal—because not based on an adequate showing of probably cause—the search is also illegal, and evidence discovered by it is thus inadmissible. The developing standards for warrants are illustrated by the following cases:

- Search warrant, to be valid, must be based on affidavit that sets forth factual details (not mere conclusions of police) that show probable cause. Affidavit merely stating that a "reliable informer" had provided "information" that narcotics were located on property to be searched was not enough to support a warrant; affidavit should have set forth facts from which *magistrate* could determine whether the informant was "reliable" and whether the information supplied did adequately support conclusion that narcotics would be found on premises. *Aguilar* v. *Texas*, USSCt.1964. Accord: *Spinelli* v. *United States* (1969).
- Search warrant that merely authorized police to enter premises and make a search for generally described material (e.g., books and pamphlets relating to Communist Party operations) was illegal, since it did not "particularly describe" the "things to be seized", as required by the Fourth Amendment. General warrants are outlawed in both state and federal proceedings. *Stanford* v. *Texas*, USSCt.1965.
- Search of buildings for evidence of health or safety violations must be based on a valid warrant, just as in criminal investigation cases; the right of privacy is just as important where enforcement of building, housing and safety codes are concerned. BUT, in light of the less drastic nature of such inspections and the necessity for making them on an area-wide basis in the interest of public health and safety, individual search warrants are not always needed. Area-wide warrants may be issued on a showing that there has been an area-wide dete-

rioration or dilapidation of housing, or an area-wide infestation of a particular health menace (e.g., rats or vermin), etc. In light of the limited purpose and effect of the desired entry (i.e., health and welfare rather than criminal law enforcement), such a showing would constitute an adequate basis for "probably cause" to issue the area-wide warrant. *Camara* v. *Municipal Court* (1967).

f. *EXCEPTIONS: Valid searches without a warrant*— are recognized in certain typical situations:

- *Consent:* If the individual whose right of privacy is threatened gives a voluntary consent to the intrusion, this amounts to a waiver of the 4th Amendment right. Similarly, if the place being searched is one shared jointly by the defendant and a third person, the latter's consent will make the search valid so that evidence of crime by the defendant—produced by the search so consented to—is admissible.

Example: Surreptitious recording of conversation with suspect by police agent *held* not violation of Fourth Amendment, since recorder merely heard what agent had heard and could have testified to (although less reliably than recording); and there was no improper or unauthorized "eavesdropping", since defendant consented to conversation with agent. *Lopez* v. *United States*, USSCt.1963.

Example: Testimony of an informer who was present in defendant's hotel room on invitation of defendant, as to incriminating statements made there by defendant, is admissible, and not violative of 4th

Amendment. Under these circumstances, defendant did not rely on privacy of hotel room to protect against disclosure, but relied on misplaced confidence in the informer. Fourth Amendment only protects the former interest in physical privacy. *Hoffa* v. *United States* (1966).

Example: Testimony of undercover police agent who obtained access to defendant's home by false representations (i.e., he posed as a willing buyer of narcotics) may testify as to incriminating events observed therein. This does not, *per se*, violate Fourth Amendment, although the agent would exceed the constitutional limits if he proceeded to make an unreasonable search of private papers, or engaged in surreptitious eavesdropping on private conversations, after he gained access. *Lewis* v. *United States* (1966).

BUT NOTE: the consent must be given freely and voluntarily—

Example: officers announced to owner of house, with whom defendant lived, that they had a warrant to search the place. She told them to "go ahead". No warrant was ever read or shown her, and none was proved at the trial. The search produced incriminating evidence that was used to convict defendant. *HELD:* Reversed. Consent secured by official claim that a warrant for a search exists is not a valid consent, for such an official claim is inherently coercive and implies no right to withhold consent to the search. Apparent consent under these circumstances is not freely and voluntarily given, but amounts to mere acquiescence to apparent legal compulsion. Hence, the evidence was improperly admitted since illegally seized under 4th Amendment. *Bumper* v. *North Carolina*, SupCt 1968.

- Valid Arrest of defendant will support a reasonable search of the immediate vicinity, and of the defendant's person, without a warrant. Evidence so discovered is admissible, since the search is regarded as reasonable, in that it is supported by a need to determine whether the defendant has secreted on him or under his immediate control any weapons with which he may try to escape, or which he may use against the arresting officer; and to take into custody any evidence of crime which the arrested person may try to destroy.

Example: Following a valid arrest based on probable cause to believe defendant had committed a felony, police officers searched the entire house, including drawers in furniture, for about an hour and found some incriminating evidence. HELD: The evidence is inadmissible, since the search went well beyond the limited area under the defendant's immediate control when he was arrested—the area in which he might, by a sudden movement, seize a gun or other weapon, or seize and destroy some evidence. To conduct a valid search beyond this narrow area the police should have sought and obtained a search warrant. *Chimel* v. *California* (1969). (Note: earlier cases—notably *Rabinowitz* v. *United States* (1959)—are expressly overruled so far as they seem to authorize a wider search in such arrest cases.)

NOTE WELL: The arrest must be a valid one—either under a valid arrest warrant or based on probably cause to believe the defendant has committed a crime. Mere suspicion does not constitute probable cause that will support such an arrest. *Beck* v. *Ohio*

(1965). Likewise, suspicious circumstances (such as large numbers of persons congregating at a private home) plus tip of an informer who is not shown to be reliable doesn't constitute probable cause to believe illegal gambling is going on to justify an arrest and search in conjunction therewith. *Recznik* v. *City of Lorain* (1968). Circumstances plus the tip of an informer shown to be reliable or based on detailed information known to the informer, however, will justify the arrest—and the prosecution need not produce the informer for cross-examination or even name him, as long as it satisfies the court that he was sufficiently reliable that his "tip" could support probably cause to make the arrest. *McCray* v. *Illinois* (1967).

- *Emergency situations:* A search and seizure without a warrant may be justified as "reasonable" and thus not a violation of the 4th Amendment if there is need for immediate action, and not enough time to apply for and secure a search warrant.

Example: Automobiles and other vehicles can be searched without a warrant, if there is probable cause to believe that incriminating evidence will be found, but only because such vehicles can easily be moved out of the locality while a warrant is being sought.

Example: Emergency doctrine, which justifies search without a warrant when time to get a warrant is not available, includes searches in "hot pursuit." Hence, search of house, based on eye-witness' statement that armed robber had just entered house, is not unreasonable in effort to capture robber and to locate weapons he might use against police or to try to effect escape. *Warden* v. *Hayden* (1967).

Example: Compulsory taking of blood sample for intoxication test, against defendant's consent, *HELD* valid, under 4th Amendment standards, where (a) preceded by valid arrest based on probable cause to believe defendant had been driving while drunk—he exhibited normal outward manifestations of intoxication, and (b) it was impracticable to secure a search warrant, since blood alcohol content tends to dissipate rapidly as body absorbs and oxidizes it. *Schmerber* v. *California* (1966).

Example: Evidence seized by police on public street after "stop and frisk" technique applied, was introduced at trial to convict. *HELD:* Convictions affirmed. "Stop-and-frisk" is constitutionally valid when (a) tested by objective man approach, rather than by police officer's subjective good faith beliefs, (b) probable cause existed for making a further investigation of individual acting in a suspicious fashion, although not to the point that a valid arrest could be affected, (c) the officer also had reasonable grounds to believe the person stopped was armed and potentially dangerous to the officer or to the public, and (d) the search is by "frisk", that is, by patting or running the hands over the outer clothing, for the purpose of locating any weapons in the person's possession. The need to get a search warrant is excused by the necessity for an immediate investigation, hence an emergency situation in which time to get a warrant is not available. On balance of interest, a stop-and-frisk approach that conforms to the indicated standards outweighs the incidental interference with personal liberty that results, and is necessary to promote effective crime prevention and detection. *Terry* v. *Ohio.* SupCt 1968.

NOTE: In companion case *Sibron* v. *New York,* held that narcotics conviction is *reversed,* where police obtained package of narcotics by search of defendant's pocket which did not meet the standards of the Terry case (i.e., no probable cause to stop and frisk, and no reason to suspect the person stopped was armed and dangerous).

4. Double Jeopardy: Right to Be Tried but Once for Same Crime:

a. In Federal prosecutions, the Double Jeopardy Clause of the 5th Amendment grants a three-fold protection: (1) D cannot be tried again for the same offense after being once tried and *acquitted.* (2) D cannot be tried a second time for the same offense after conviction. (3) D cannot be punished more than once for a single offense.
b. What is "double jeopardy" and when has accused been put in "jeopardy"?

- Second trial for same act not prohibited, merely second trial for the same offense.

Example: D was tried on indictment charging both 1st and 2nd degree murder, and was found guilty of 2nd degree only. On appeal, judgment was reversed for insufficiency of evidence. U.S. prosecutor (in the District of Columbia) then tried D again on the 1st degree murder charge, with the result that D was convicted. Held: reversed—the jury in the first trial found D guilty only of 2nd degree murder, thus implying him innocent of 1st degree murder. To retry him thus violates double jeopardy clause, even though reversal of the first judgment was secured at request of D. *Green* v. *United States*, USSCt. 1957.

- If D is convicted a second time in a permissible retrial for the same offense (*e.g.*, following a successful appeal or collateral attack on the first conviction), the Double Jeopardy Clause requires that full credit be given for all time served under the first sentence in reduction of time required to be served under the new sentence. To deny such credit is, in effect, to punish D twice. *North Carolina* v. *Pearce* (1969).

BUT NOTE: The trial court, in determining the second sentence, is permitted to impose a *more severe penalty* than the original sentence, if warranted by objective circumstances concerning identifiable conduct of the defendant since the time of original sentencing, which is relevant to sentencing policy. However, it would violate Due Process to impose a more severe penalty as a deterrent to challenging convictions, or for reasons of malice or retaliation. To preclude such improper motives on resentencing, the trial judge must disclose on the record the factual reasons for any increased punishment he imposes, with their evidentiary support, so that judicial review may be available to assure that only constitutionally permissible factors were considered. *North Carolina* v. *Pearce* (1969).

QUERY: The Court does not discuss, and thus leaves open, the questions as to whether the foregoing rules are applicable where a state has an indeterminate sentence law (as in California), and if so, what procedural mechanisms will be required to assure that D is actually given full credit for previous time served, and is given an increased sentence only for permissible reasons.

- Jeopardy applies not only for the offense for which the accused is first indicted, but for all necessarily included offenses.

  BUT: "Necessarily included offenses" is very strictly interpreted and if any element of one crime is different from any element of the other crime, double jeopardy is eliminated.

Example: Abortion and murder are not necessarily included crimes, because death is not an element of abortion, even though the homicide in question occurred as a result of abortion.

Example: D was tried for murder of wife, and sentenced to 30 years. Subsequently he was tried for murder of child #1, and again sentenced to 30 years. Subsequently he was tried for murder of child #2, and sentenced to death. All three murders occurred at same time, and evidence of all three was introduced at all three trials. HELD: death sentence affirmed, for the state could rationally treat the three murders as separate and disctinct crimes, hence no basic unfairness to try D three separate times. (*Ciucci* v. *Illinois*, U.S. Sup.Ct., 1958).

- Double jeopardy does not preclude a civil suit for penalties against one acquitted of a criminal charge on the same facts.
- Jeopardy does not attach in a jury trial until the jury is sworn; in a non-jury trial, the trial must be commenced or "entered upon." BUT: Jeopardy cannot attach unless a court had jurisdiction.
- Whether discontinuance of a trial without reaching a verdict amounts to being once in jeopardy, depends on the particular circumstances. *Example:* Mistrial, due to disqualification of a juror, or due to a "hung jury" does not preclude a retrial.

c. *In state prosecutions,* the Double Jeopardy Clause is deemed fully applicable against the states as part of the Due Process required by the Fourteenth Amendment. *Benton* v. *Maryland* (1969), overruling *Palko* v. *Connecticut.*

Example: D was charged with (1) larceny and (2) burglary, and after trial, was acquitted of larceny but convicted of burglary. On appeal, conviction reversed. State then retried D on both counts (1) and (2), and he was convicted on both charges. HELD: Larceny convictions must be reversed as a violation of Double Jeopardy, as applied to states under Due Process Clause. *Benton* v. *Maryland* (1969).

NOTE ALSO: In *Benton,* the fact that D had been given *concurrent* sentences did not preclude Sup.Ct from reviewing the larceny conviction, on which the shorter sentence was given, since this conviction, if unreversed, could have adverse collateral consequences for D in later years (e.g., it might be used to impose more severe punishment for recidivism; or to impeach credibility of D as a witness, etc.) Hence, not moot.

NOTE ALSO: In *Benton*, after vacating the larceny conviction, the court also reversed the buglary conviction and remanded to the state court to determine whether the buglary conviction had been influenced unconstitutionally by receipt and consideration by the jury of evidence relating to the improper larceny charge.

d. *The Dual Sovereignties Rule:* In past decisions, the Court has held that the Double Jeopardy Clause only forbids a second prosecution (or punishment) by the *same* sovereign government. Thus, a previous conviction (or acquittal) in a state prosecution will not bar a later federal prosecution for the same offense. (Note: Some acts are crimes under both state and federal law—e.g., bank robbery, kidnapping, etc.) Or vice versa. See *Abbate* v. *United States* (1959); *Bartkus* v. *Illinois* (1959).

NOTE WELL: Now that the Double Jeopardy Clause has been fully incorporated into the Fourteenth Amendment, this "dual sovereignties" concept makes little sense, and could be employed to frustrate the protection of the Clause. It is probable that the Court will overrule it at the earliest opportunity to do so. NOTE: The similar "dual sovereignties" theory which was once the law under the privilege against self-incrimination—for example, the rule formerly was that a witness in a *state* trial could not claim the privilege against self-incrimination if the only fear was that of *federal* prosecution—has long been overruled. *Murphy* v. *Waterfront Commission* (1964).

5. *Incrimination by Testimonial Compulsion: Privilege against Self-Incrimination:*

a. *Federal and state* requirements are identical:
   Prior cases to the contrary have been overruled—it is now settled that the privilege against self-incrimination is included as one of the rights protected by the Due Process Clause of the 14th Amendment against state impairment, as well as by Fifth Amendment against federal impairment. The standards of application of the privilege are the same in both state and federal proceedings—the federal constitutional standard. *Malloy* v. *Hogan*, USSCt. 1964.
b. *Effect of an immunity statute:*
   The privilege may be circumvented by grant of an immunity which is coextensive with the scope of the privilege—that is, which removes the danger of prosecution for any crime disclosed by the compelled testimony or by any evidence discovered as a result of the compelled testimony. *Counselman* v. *Hitchcock*, USSCt. 1892.

Congress may validly enact an immunity statute which immunizes a federal witness from both federal and state prosecution based on his compelled testimony. Thus the rule of *Counselman* v. *Hitchcock*, supra, may be satisfied in federal proceedings by a properly drawn statute. *Ullmann* v. *United States*, USSCt. 1956.

BUT NOTE: The immunity statute must be explicit and comprehensive enough to fully supplant the protection given by the privilege.

Example: Individual members of Communist Party cannot be required to register under Internal Security Act, since the very act of filing a registration form constitutes an admission of Party membership and thus presents a threat of criminal prosecution under Smith Act. Nor does the fact that the Government already *knows* the individual persons being prosecuted for non-registration are Party members make any difference. The judgment whether a disclosure is "incriminating" does not depend upon an assessment of the extent of the Government's information at the time of the interrogation; to hold that it does would seriously impair the privilege by surrounding it with grave uncertainties from the viewpoint of the person invoking it. Only a comprehensive immunity from prosecution will suffice to preclude exercise of the privilege; and the mere statutory declaration that the fact of registration cannot be received in evidence against the Party member doesn't preclude use of the registration statement as an investigatory lead, hence the protection is not sufficiently comprehensive. The registration requirement is thus unconstitutional. *Albertson* v. *Subversive Activities Control Board*, SupCt. Nov. 1965.

c. *Dual sovereignties doctrine:*

The constitutional privilege protects a state witness against incrimination under *either* state *or* federal law. Likewise, it protects a federal witness from incrimination under *either* state *or* federal law. *Murphy* v. *Waterfront Commission*, USSCt. 1964.

In order to implement the rule that a state witness may assert the privilege against self-incrimination, where he fears federal prosecution as a result of his testimony, and yet still provide ample opportunity for state criminal law investigations, the Supreme Court has adopted the rule that any testimony obtained from a state witness under a state immunity statute cannot be employed (nor can its "fruits" be employed) to convict the witness in a federal prosecution. Thus state immunity statutes may still be given effect without violating the privilege as to fear of federal prosecutions. *Murphy* v. *Waterfront Commission*, USSCt.1964.

d. *Scope of the privilege against self-incrimination:* Testimonial compulsion is the object of the privilege; hence, the privilege is not violated by a compulsory blood test (*Schmerber* v. *California*, 1966), compulsory taking of handwriting exemplar for analysis by expert (*Gilbert* v. *California*, 1967), or by forcing an accused to provide physical evidence (exhibit his person, try on clothing, speak to demonstrate tone and pitch of voice, etc.). *United States* v. *Wade* (1967). None of these instances amount to the extraction of *thoughts*, either verbal or written, from the defendant, which might tend to expose him to the risk of prosecution or provide leads to the discovery of evidence that would do so.

BUT COMPARE: Statute that requires a citizen to file a written statement containing information that might provide a lead to possible criminal prosecution, or which by its very filing would tend to identify the person filing it as one who may be guilty of possible criminal activities, is subject to the privilege. Thus, a person subject thereto who fails to file cannot be criminally prosecuted for his failure, if he asserts his privilege against self-incrimination at the trial; the privilege under these circumstances is an absolute defense (absent a valid immunity statute).

Example: Registration requirement of federal gambling tax law violates self-incrimination, since registration exposes gambler (or one who contemplates gambling in future) to risk of prosecution under state law, where registration statements are matters of public record. *Marchetti* v. *United States* (1968). Ditto as to registration requirement under federal tax on sawed-off shotguns and submachine guns. *Haynes* v. *United States* (1968). And as to Communist Party membership registration requirement of Internal Security Act. *Albertson* v. *SACB* (1965), *supra.* And as to registration requirements connected with administration of marijuana transfer tax law. *Leary* v. *United States* (1969).

e. *No comment rule:* Comment by judge or prosecutor on defendant's failure to testify in his own behalf, thereby inviting jury to consider his silence as bearing upon the question of guilt, violates the privilege.

Example: California statute permits prosecutor and judge to comment to jury in criminal case about defendant's failure to take witness stand and testify in his own behalf, even though defendant's decision not to do so may be motivated largely by corollary rule that if he does take the witness stand, his testimony may be impeached by proof of prior convictions (which evidence would otherwise be inadmissible). HELD: Unconstitutional conditioning of privilege against self-incrimination which is now regarded as incorporated into Due Process Clause of 14th Amendment. The fact that the jury might draw adverse inferences from the defendant's silence in any event does not mean that comment is non-prejudicial. Such comment tends to emphasize and distort the defendant's silence, and may induce jury to give it more significance than would be appropriate. Hence, such comment denies the defendant a fair trial. *Adamson* v. California is overruled. *Griffin* v. *California*, SupCt. April 1965.

f. *Relationship to right of counsel:* The *Miranda* Doctrine—see discussion, *supra*, under topic of COUNSEL, RIGHT TO—is designed to give effective protection to the privilege against self-incrimination, by providing assurance that a suspect will not respond to police interrogation without full knowledge of his privilege, and of his right to have an attorney to advise him and assist in applying the privilege where appropriate in the course of police interrogation.
g. *Assertion of the privilege as basis for civil sanctions:*

Assertion of the privilege against self-incrimination may not be the basis for a conclusive presumption of guilt, without regard for relevant circumstances, possible justification for the assertion, or possible extenuating circumstances under which claim of privilege may be consistent with innocence. To so employ the privilege violates Due Process. *Slochower* v. *Board of Education*, USSCt. 1956.

BUT COMPARE: refusal to answer question relevant to fitness for public employment—even though couched in terms of privilege against self-incrimination—may be made a ground of discharge from employment, where employee was ordered to answer as part of his duties by his employer and his refusal thus constituted "insubordination". *Nelson* v. *County of Los Angeles*, USSCt.1960.

NOTE WELL: The *Nelson* case—and others like it—have been undercut by recent decisions that indicate that civil-type sanctions are of doubtful constitutionality when they are imposed as a penalty for invocation of the privilege. These cases did not overrule the *Nelson* line of cases, but their rationale is clearly closer to *Slochower*. Consider: *Garrity* v. *New Jersey* (1967): conviction of police officer for fixing traffic tickets was based, in part, upon use of confession given in course of official investigation. A statute required all policemen to be discharged forthwith if, under such circumstances, policeman refused to answer questions relating to his official conduct. Garrity chose to confess rather than "take the 5th" and be discharged. *Held:* The threat of loss of employment if the constitutional privilege was asserted constitutes coercion and duress which vitiates confession and precludes any conclusion of waiver of the privilege. Hence, confession was inadmissible in prosecution of officer.

Spevack v. *Klein* (1967): An attorney cannot be disbarred for asserting privilege against self-incrimination in official investigation of "ambulance chasing." To use the constitutional privilege as a ground for disbarment burdens the exercise of a constitutional right. Attorneys have the same constitutional rights as other citizens.

Gardner v. *Broderick* (1968) and *Uniformed Sanitation Men* v. *NYC* (1968): City employees (sanitation employees, and a policeman) were discharged because they refused to waive their privilege against self-incrimination and to sign a waiver of immunity from criminal prosecution based on evidence they might be compelled to give in investigations into official corruption. *HELD:* Discharges are invalid. The state cannot constitutionally compel a public employee to make the choice between losing his job or waiving his constitutional protection against criminal prosecution.

Query: Could city discharge on "insubordination" grounds if employee asserted privilege, where immunity statute afforded full protection against criminal prosecution?

6. *Indictment by Grand Jury: Right To, in Criminal Prosecutions:*

a. In *federal* cases, the Fifth Amendment guarantees that every accusation for an infamous crime (i.e. one punishable by imprisonment in a penitentiary) shall be by indictment.
   - The indictment must be by a regularly impanelled grand jury. *Hence, if certain segments of population have been systematically excluded in selecting grand jury*, indictment is void.
   - The constitutional right is infringed if the indictment does not state with particularity the elements of the offense charged.
   - *Exception:* Indictment is not necessary to institute prosecution for criminal contempt of court (where penalty may be several years im-

prisonment, in court's discretion) for contempt is an historical exception to the rule. (*Green* v. *United States*, U.S. Sup. Ct., 1958).

b. In *state* cases, the indictment procedure is not required to be followed, for this guarantee has *not* been incorporated into 14th Amendment.
   - Thus, state prosecutions instituted by information are permissible under due process. (*Hurtado* v. *California*, U.S. Sup. Ct., 1884). NOTE, HOWEVER: The due process clause does guarantee that the defendant will receive, in some form, adequate prior notice of the offense for which he is to be tried.

7. *Public and Speedy Trial:*

a. In *federal* cases, the Sixth Amendment guarantees the defendant a public trial. The Superior Court has not yet explicitly decided to what extent this forbids trial judge from excluding spectators, but Circuit Courts have been strict.
   - *Example:* In rape case, order excluding all spectators except relatives and newsmen HELD void, where made to prevent embarrassment of prosecuting witness. (*Tanksley* v. *U.S.*, 9th Cir. 1944).

b. In *state* cases, the right to a public trial is regarded as included in due process under 14th Amendment, but the degree of incorporation is not clear. Secret proceedings at least are forbidden.
   - *Example:* Criminal contempt conviction of witness before "one-man grand jury" HELD void on ground the proceeding was secretly conducted. (In re *Oliver*, U.S. Sup. Ct., 1948).

c. *Speedy trial must also be assured*, so that accused is not exposed indefinitely to embarrassment, scorn and contempt while under criminal charges that may be unfounded, and to preclude the accused from being deprived of freedom of travel and to engage in normal business activities because of need to remain in readiness to defend against prosecution when ultimately expedited. *Klopfer* v. *North Carolina* (1967).

Example: Prisoner serving a sentence in a federal prison in State A is entitled to a speedy trial under state charges pending in State B and failure of state to undertake a diligent good-faith effort to bring him to trial (necessarily requiring cooperation of federal prison authorities in making defendant available for trial in State B) will entitle defendant to dismissal of charges in State B. *Smith* v. *Hooey* (1969) (court notes that even a prisoner may sustain serious harm from delay in trial under other charges: possible loss of chance for concurrent, rather than consecutive, sentence; possible ineligibility for parole or for diminished sentence while criminal charges are pending against prisoner; psychological impact making rehabilitation less likely; inability to provide an adequate defense even if innocent).

8. *Confrontation and Cross-Examination of Prosecution Witnesses:*

a. In *federal* cases, these rights are guaranteed by the Sixth Amendment.

BUT NOTE: these rights are not necessarily required in administrative investigatory proceedings. *Hannan* v. *Larche*, U.S. Sup. Ct., 1960, so holding, as to Federal Civil Rights Commission, on ground the Commission merely investigated and did not adjudicate; trial-type procedures would undoubtedly hamper or frustrate the investigatory purposes of the Commission; and informal investigatory procedures have been historically accepted.

COMPARE: If the investigatory agency does more than merely find facts and make a report or recommend legislative action—if it, for example, is charged by law with duty to determine "guilt" as an auxiliary agency to criminal law enforcement proceedings—the right of confrontation and cross-examination must be given. *Jenkins* v. *McKeithen* (1969), distinguishing *Hannah* v. *Larche.*

b. *In state cases*, the right to confront and cross-examine is fully incorporated as part of Due Process, for this right is deemed essential to the search for truth in that it provides the traditionally vindicated techniques of the adversary system for testing the credibility of incriminating evidence.

Example: Principal prosecution witness testified under false name of "James Jordan". The trial judge refused to permit defense counsel to question the witness as to his true name and address. *HELD:* Denial of right to cross-examine as to true name and address effectively emasculates the defendant's ability to test the credibility of the witness, and thus denies due process since the starting point for penetrating cross-examination is to determine the witness' true identity. *Smith* v. *State of Illinois*, SupCt 1968.

Example: During course of trial, deputy sheriff in charge of jury made derogatory remarks about the defendant to members of the jury. HELD: Conviction must be reversed, since jury might have been influenced by deputy sheriff's statements, or may think the deputy has "inside" official information about the defendant which they should evaluate; yet the deputy was never subject to confrontation and cross-examination. *Parker* v. *Gladden* (1966).

Example: In joint trial of A and B, confession of defendant A, which implicated defendant B, was introduced subject to instruction that jury should consider it only as bearing on guilt of A. *HELD:* B's conviction reversed. Despite the limiting instruction, the use of the confession violated B's right to confront and cross-examine; the jury may have considered the confession against B anyway, since it is psychologically impossible for the jury to wipe the confession from its mind when it considers the issue of B's guilt, while considering it as against A, in a joint trial of both defendants. Since A did not testify, B had no opportunity to cross-examine him and thus test the credibility of the incriminating statements in the confession. *Bruton* v. *United States*, SupCt 1968.

c. *Excuse or waiver:* Extent of the constitutional right to confront and cross-examine may depend to some extent on circumstances, subject to balancing of competing interests.

Example: Defendant's Oklahoma robbery conviction was based principally upon the recorded testimony (read into evidence at trial) of adverse witness given at preliminary hearing. The witness had not then been cross-examined by defendant's counsel; and, at the time of trial, the witness was serving time in federal prison in Texas. *Held:* The only excuse for not presenting an adverse witness in person, to be confronted and cross-examined by defendant, is where the witness is actually unavailable or dead. But here the state made no effort to try to secure attendance of the missing witness, although procedures were available by which he might have been produced, subject to discretion of federal prison officers. Defendant's failure to cross-examine at the preliminary is not a waiver of his right to do so at the trial, for defendant had no reason to anticipate that the witness would not be produced at the trial, and a preliminary is a far less searching examination than a trial in any event. Thus, defendant was denied constitutional right to confront accusing witness and cross-examine him, under 6th Amendment as incorporated into 14th. *Barber* v. *Page*, SupCt 1968.

Example: A waiver of the right to confront and cross-examine will not be inferred from either silence in the record, or even from apparent waiver by counsel. This right is so important that a waiver will not be deemed to have taken place unless the record shows a clear and intentional acquiescence in the waiver by the defendant *personally*, with understanding of what he is doing. *Brookhart* v. *Janis* (1966).

9. *Bail, Right to Reasonable:*

a. In *federal* cases, which do not involve capital punishment, under Eighth Amendment, the defendant is entitled to be released on bail fixed at a figure no higher than reasonably necessary to ensure his presence at the trial. (*Stack* v. *Boyle*, U.S.Sup.Ct., 1951). In capital offenses, admission to bail and the amount thereof are discretionary with trial judge.

In *state* cases, the Superior Court has never regarded the right to bail as part of due process—and one case held that denial of bail pending appeal was *not* violative of 14th Amendment. (*McKane Durston*, U.S. Sup.Ct., 1894).

10. *Cruel and Unusual Punishment, Right to be Free From:*

a. In *federal* cases, the 8th Amendment ensures that the punishment will not involve wanton infliction of pain, and that it will not be grossly disproportionate to the gravity of the offense.
   (1) *Example:* Sentence of 20 years at hard labor in chains, as punishment for falsification of public record, HELD void. (*Weems* v. *United States*, U.S. Sup.Ct., 1910).
b. In *state* cases, Due Process includes guarantee against cruel and unusual punishment. For example, to punish a person who is sick (i.e., a narcotics addict), where no evidence of illegal *conduct* is shown, violates Due Process as cruel punishment. *Robinson* v. *California*, USSCt. 1962.

BUT COMPARE: *Is chronic alcoholism punishable as a crime?*

Defendant, a chronic alcoholic, was convicted of being drunk in a public place. He had been convicted of drunkenness many times before. *HELD:* Conviction affirmed. This is not a violation of the cruel and unusual punishment clause of 8th Amendment as included in 14th. On balance of interests, public drunk convictions are not the same as convictions for narcotic addiction (which was deemed cruel and unusual punishment in Robinson v. California) since (a) Medical evidence is inconclusive as to whether drunkenness and alcoholism are medical illnesses or behavioral disorders. (b) To declare such convictions and arrests to be unconstitutional would merely turn thousands of drunks out of jail to be on the street, where they may be dangerous to themselves and to others, and a prey to criminal elements; society simply doesn't have the treatment facilities necessary to handle the volume of drunk cases if they can't be handled in jails. Arrests at least protect the alcoholic person while he sobers up. (c) The crime in question is not, like narcotics addiction, based purely on a status, but is based on being drunk in a public place, thus punishing the behavioral aspect of the alcoholism rather than the physiological condition alone. *Powell* v. *Texas*, SupCt 1968. (Note: This is only a plurality opinion, by 4 justices. White concurs on ground (c), but denies that state may make chronic alcoholism, without more, a crime. Fortas, Douglas, Brennan, and Stewart dissent.)

11. *Process, Right to Compulsory Process to Obtain Defense Witnesses:*

In both federal and state criminal prosecutions, the right to compulsory process to secure defense witnesses (as secured by Sixth Amendment) must be accorded to the defendant.

Example: During his trial under a murder charge, pursuant to a Texas statute, defendant was denied the right to call as a witness in his behalf a person previously tried and convicted as a coparticipant in the same murder. *HELD:* Conviction reversed, since denial of the right to call a physically and mentally competent eyewitness, whose testimony would have been relevant and material, denies defendant the right to compulsory process to obtain witnesses in his favor. This right, expressed in the Sixth Amendment, is fundamental to a fair trial and this is incorporated as part of the Due Process that states are required to give criminal defendants. *Washington* v. *Texas* (1967).

NOTE: This decision does *not* throw doubt upon the validity of evidentiary privileges, such as the attorney-client or husband-wife privileges, which are based on substantive policy considerations.

12. *Due Process of Law:* The Due Process Clauses of the 5th and 14th Amendments constitute independent constitutional requirements which both state and federal criminal proceedings must satisfy. This Due Process ground is usually invoked by the Court to set aside a criminal conviction for reasons that do not fit neatly within one of the specifically enumerated grounds discussed above: its essence is that criminal proceedings must conform to fundamental notions of fair play and substantial justice.

The principal lines of relevant decisions under the independent Due Process ground include the following:

a. *Evidence must not be obtained by means of physical abuse:* Where evidence is obtained by methods which are abhorrent to civilized justice, and which unreasonably violate the freedom of the individual from unconsented invasions of his body, such evidence cannot be used to convict despite the fact that it is reliable and trustworthy.
Example: Evidence obtained by pumping stomach of defendant over his continuous and violent protest cannot be used to convict, for such police practice is too close to the rack and screw to be regarded as Due Process. (*Rochin* v. *California*, U.S. Sup.Ct., 1952).
COMPARE: Evidence obtained by chemical analysis of blood of defendant extracted from him by acceptable medical procedure and by trained medical personnel while he was unconscious, held, may be used to convict, since simple blood test is common and painless medical procedure, and alcohol blood test is a scientifically accurate test for drunkenness which tends to protect the innocent against unjust conviction and to deter drinkers from driving, thereby being justified by need to cut down on slaughter on the highways. (*Breithaupt* v. *Abram*, U.S. Sup.Ct., 1957). NOTE: Same result where the blood test was taken by compulsion, over defendant's objection, by competent medical personnel under circumstances not amounting to brutality and designed to minimize pain and discomfort. *Schmerber* v. *California* (1966).

b. *Coerced or involuntary confessions:* Use in evidence of confessions obtained by duress, promises of leniency, fraud, collusion, or psychological trickery (and which thus are not free and voluntary) violates due process. Policy: to deter unlawful police practices; and to conform our system of justice to civilized standards which will command respect.

- The Supreme Court, in cases where it is alleged that a coerced confession was employed in evidence, is not bound by the determination of the jury that the confession was voluntary. In order to protect constitutional rights, the court must itself re-examine the evidence. If there is a substantial conflict in the evidence on coercion, the determination of the trier of fact will normally be left undisturbed. BUT IF the court finds from the *undisputed or uncontradicted* portions of the evidence that there is a reasonable PROBABILITY that the confession was not voluntary, its use constitutes a denial of Due Process of the Law.

Example: Uneducated Negro of low mentality, charged with attempted rape of white woman, was held in isolation for one week, during which time he was questioned repeatedly by police but was not permitted to see friends, relatives or an attorney. *HELD:* although there is no evidence of physical brutality, confession secured in this setting violates due process. Conviction based thereon is reversed. *Fikes* v. *Alabama*, Jan. 1957. 77 Sup Ct 281.

Example: Confession secured from robbery suspect after prolonged interrogation in tiny room by relays of police officers held inadmissible as violation of due process, where the uncontradicted evidence "indisutably establishes the strongest probability" that defendant was insane at the time of his questioning and confession, and that confession was thus not the voluntary act of a free and intelligent mind. Court points out that the test of Due Process is one of appraising the "totality of circumstances", and that whether such circumstances had an effect on the defendant's "independence of will" was always, by its nature, a question of "probabilities". (*Blackburn* v. *Alabama*, U.S. Sup. Ct., 1960).

Example: Murder suspect, who was a drug addict, was given medication for withdrawal symptoms, mixed with a "truth serum". While under the influence of these drugs, defendant confessed in response to police questioning, and the confession was used to convict him. No evidence of coercion. *HELD:* Denial of due process, for a drug-induced confession is not a product of free will and hence is constitutionally inadmissible. *Townsend* v. *Sain*, USSCt. 1963.

- *Fruit of the poisonous tree doctrine:* Exculpatory evidence induced by a constitutionally inadmissible confession is also inadmissible.
  Example: In a prior trial, D had testified in an effort to explain away a confession used by the prosecutor. The conviction had been reversed and the confession held inadmissible. At the present retrial the prosecutor read defendant's previous testimony to the jury. *HELD:* Conviction reversed. The prior damaging testimony was induced by a desire to overcome the impact of the confession, by trying to explain plaintiff's actions in a way consistent with innocence or at least a reduced charge. Hence, it was the fruit of the poisonous tree, and equally excludable. *Harrison* v. *U.S.*, SupCt 1968.
- *Truth or falsity of a confession are irrelevant* to its constitutional admissibility. The issue is whether the confession is the product of ex-

traneous influences—coercive or inducing in nature—which produce a confession that is not free and voluntary. Even a thoroughly truthful and completely corroborated confession is constitutionally inadmissible if secured by methods which Due Process condemns—for, in effect, such a confession constitutes a compulsory extraction from the defendant of self-incriminatory matter in violation of his constitutional right to remain silent. *Rogers* v. *Richmond*, USSCt. 1961.

- *Procedure required* in use of confession at trial: Due Process considerations of fairness require that, in both state and federal trials, confessions challenged as being involuntary must be *first* presented to the judge, in the absence of the jury. The judge must then decide, *independently and as an issue of fact* on the evidence, whether the confession was involuntary. IF JUDGE FINDS IT WAS INVOLUNTARY, the confession cannot be submitted to the jury for any purpose, so as not to infect the jury's deliberations of the merits. IF JUDGE FINDS IT WAS VOLUNTARY, he should then submit the confesssion to the jury, with proper instructions, leaving the ultimate issue of whether it was voluntary or not to the jury if state law so provides—and the jury may then disagree with the judge, and find the confession to be involuntary, and hence disregard it. *Jackson* v. *Denno*, USSCt. 1964.

c. *Knowing use by prosecutor of false, misleading or perjured testimony:* Where the State knowingly uses evidence which it knows to be false, or deliberately suppresses evidence known to it which the defendant does not know and which materially affects the significance of the evidence presented by the prosecution, Due Process is violated by conviction based thereon.

Example: Defendant was convicted of murder chiefly on testimony of an accomplice. Although the prosecutor had in fact promised leniency to the accomplice in return for his testimony, at the trial he asked and permitted the witness to state that no such consideration had been promised. *HELD:* conviction reversed. The knowing use of perjured testimony violates Due Process, even where as here it goes only to possible impeachment of credibility of a witness and not to the facts of the alleged offense. *Napue* v. *Illinois*, 70 Sup. Ct., 1173 (1959).

Example: In trial of defendant for murder (with death sentence as result), prosecutor suppressed confession given by co-defendant that co-defendant had actually been the one who committed the killing—thus tending to show that defendant was only an accomplice. *HELD:* Denial of due process. If disclosed, the confession would not have affected the determination of defendant's guilt—but the jury might have taken it into consideration in determining the punishment, and might have given a sentence of life imprisonment rather than death. Deliberate suppression of this evidence favorable to defendant thus requires a new trial on the issue of punishment. *Brady* v. *Maryland*, USSCt. 1963.

Example: Defendant sentenced to death for murder of his wife, claimed as a defense that he had killed her in sudden justifiable heat of anger on seeing her kissing W. If believed, this defense would result in maximum sentence of 5 years imprisonment. Prosecutor at trial permitted W. to testify that he and deceased were only friends, and deliberately withheld and concealed testimony of W., known to prosecutor, to effect that W. and decedent had engaged in prolonged illicit relationship. *HELD:* since the concealed evidence tended to support D's defense, its deliberate concealment by prosecutor constituted denial of Due Process requiring reversal of conviction. *Alcorta* v. *Texas*, 78 Sup. Ct., 103 (Nov. 1957).

NOTE: Deliberate misrepresentation by prosecutor has the same effect as a denial of Due Process. Thus, in a murder case, prosecutor with reason to know that certain brown stains on undershorts were paint, permitted expert to testify in misleading way that chemical tests had established they were blood of same type as child victim's, and then repeatedly argued to jury that said "bloody shorts" linked defendant to alleged crime. In fact, later tests established (and state does not contest truth of later findings) that the stains were paint. *Held:* Denial of fair trial. *Miller* v. *Pate* (1967).

It is still not entirely clear whether the prosecutor has a duty under Due Process to disclose to the defense *all* evidence known to him which is favorable in any way to the defendant. Does any such duty arise only when the defendant makes a request? Or would it arise if the prosecutor had reason to believe that the defendant's counsel did not suspect the existence of such evidence? Would all such failures to disclose require a reversal of a conviction? See: *Giles* v. *Maryland* (1967) (conflicting dicta suggesting Court is badly divided on these issues; decision reached on non-constitutional grounds.)

d. *Judge with financial interest in convictions:* Where judge received costs only in event of conviction but not in acquittals, his personal interest in outcome renders conviction void. (*Tumey* v. *Ohio*, U.S. Sup.Ct., 1927).

e. *Mob-dominated trial:* Violates due process. (*Moore* v. *Dempsey*, U.S. Sup. Ct., 1923).

f. *Trial by newspaper or television:* When local publicity of an inflammatory nature makes it impossible to have a fair trial in the local court, a change of venue or postponement of trial is essential to ensure right to objective jury determination of guilt. Conviction under influence of such inflammatory publicity denies Due Process. *Irwin* v. *Doud*, USSCt. 1961 (trial by newspaper); *Rideau* v. *Louisiana*, USSCt. 1963 (trial by television).

Example: Murder conviction *held* denial of Due Process, where trial was surrounded by massive, pervasive and highly prejudicial publicity by all news media, and trial judge, after denying a change of venue, failed to a) adequately control activities of reporters and cameramen in courthouse and courtroom, b) adequately insulate witnesses from influences of publicity media, c) adequately exercise control over police officers, witnesses and counsel to prevent release to the media of statements, gossip, and other information, including inadmissible matter which was widely printed and thus called to the jury's attention, and d) adequately control jury's access to the mass media during the trial and during their deliberations. *Sheppard* v. *Maxwell*, SupCt. June 1966.

NOTE: In dictum, the Court suggests that trial judges should take "strong measures" to control and discipline police, attorneys and court personnel to see that surrounding publicity does not cast the balance of fairness against an accused. Here, says the court, "had the judge, the other officers of the court [including the prosecutor], and the police placed the interest of justice first, the news media would have soon learned to be content with the task of reporting the case as it unfolded in the courtroom—not pieced together from extrajudicial statements." Moreover, when a claim is made that there has been an unfair "trial by news media", the appellate courts must "make an independent evaluation of the circumstances", and cannot be bound by the lower court's evaluation of the record.

Example: Defendant's trial for swindling was highly publicized and of great public interest. Over objections of defense counsel, portions of the trial proceedings were televised, although most of the time the TV cameras were hidden behind a soundproofed partition erected in the back of the courtroom. HELD: Conviction reversed. Television coverage of actual trial proceedings, under these circumstances, denied defendant the kind of fair trial assured by Due Process Clause in light of probable distracting impact on jurors, trial judge, witnesses, defendant, and counsel.

g. *Evidence to support guilt must be introduced:* Conviction on a charge of loitering, where there was no evidence whatever in the record tending to show a violation of the statute, held to constitute a violation of Due Process, for to convict a person without introducing evidence of guilt is clearly irrational and contrary to substantial justice. (*Thompson* v. *Louisville*, U.S. Sup.Ct., 1960).

Example: Conviction of peaceful demonstrators for "disorderly conduct", where evidence merely showed that they had refused to obey a police order to disperse [note: defendants were not charged with failure to obey], HELD denial of Due Process, since no evidence of crime charged was adduced. *Gregory* v. *City of Chicago* (1969).

Example: Rev. Shuttlesworth, a civil rights leader, was convicted of refusal to obey police officer's instructions to move on, under statute making refusal a crime in connection with orders relating to control of vehicular traffic. *Held:* Reversed for violation of Due Process, where there was no evidence whatever tending to show that officer who gave order was engaged in traffice control, that defendant in any way was interfering with traffic. *Shuttlesworth* v. *City of Birmingham* (1965).

h. *Official entrapment or its equivalent:* it is a violation of Due Process for the state to lull an individual into a sense of false security or belief that his conduct or proposed course of conduct is approved by the state, or will not incur penalties—and then to apply criminal sanctions based on such conduct.

Example: Witness before legislative committee was advised that if he wished, he could refuse to answer questions on basis of state constitutional privilege against self-incrimination. Witness, in reliance on this advice, declined to answer several questions. Subsequently, the witness was convicted of contempt of the legislature for refusing to answer, since an applicable immunity statute removed his privilege against self-incrimination. HELD: conviction is violation of Due Process, amounting to a reprehensible form of entrapment of grossly unfair nature. *Raley* v. *Ohio*, USSCt. 1959.

Example: Civil rights demonstrators were marching and displaying signs near a courthouse, and were convicted under statute making it a crime to picket *near* a courthouse. When the demonstrators approached the courthouse area, the chief of police told them to stay on the opposite side of the street from the courthouse, and stated they had no objection to the assemblage if it stayed there, at least for a short period of time. HELD: conviction violates Due Process—for demonstrators were lulled into sense of security, believing that police had consented to demonstration on opposite side of street and that no crime would be committed if they did so. To convict under these circumstances is an indefensible form of entrapment. *Cox* v. *Louisiana*, USSCt. 1965.

i. *Access to courts interfered with:* State may not unreasonably interfere with rights of accused to invoke judicial protection otherwise available to him.

Example: Prison rules prohibiting prisoners from sending papers out of prison, thereby preventing timely filing of notice of appeal, held void. (*Dowd* v. *United States*, U.S.Sup.Ct.,1951).

Example: Prison regulations barring "jail-house lawyers" (i.e., other inmates) from assisting prisoners in preparing post-conviction petitions for habeas corpus HELD void, as tending to interfere with right of habeas corpus and Due Process review of validity of convictions. *Johnson* v. *Avery* (1969). (Note: The opinion implies that state may impose reasonable regulations of time, place and manner, short of prohibition.)

j. *Improperly administered jury trial:* a jury trial must be conducted in such a way as to ensure that jury's deliberations will be objective and uninfluenced by extra-judicial factors.

Example: Prime witnesses against defendant were two deputy sheriffs. After they had testified against defendant, the same two deputies were placed in charge of the jury throughout the trial, taking the jury to lunch and to the jury's hotel, and fraternizing with jurors generally. HELD: conviction reversed, as a denial of Due Process, since fraternization of witnesses with the jury in this manner was likely to affect the jury's evaluation of the witnesses' credibility and reliability, and thus unfairly influence the verdict. *Turner* v. *Louisiana*, USSCt. 1965.

k. *Mental capacity of defendant to stand trial:* The conviction of a criminal defendant while he is mentally incompetent to understand and participate in the proceedings violates Due Process. Hence, when the proceedings tend to show a substantial possibility that such incompetence actually exists, the court on its own motion is required to hold a full hearing to establish the facts. Failure to do so requires reversal of conviction so obtained. *Pate* v. *Robinson* (1966).

l. *Recidivism proceedings:* Under Texas law, the

commission of prior crimes may be charged and proved at the trial, although the jury is then instructed that priors cannot be considered in determining whether or not defendant is guilty of present offense charged. *Held:* Valid and consistent with Due Process. It must be assumed that the jury follows the instructions; and proof of priors at trial may be deemed reasonably consistent with state recidivism policy, since the jury is entitled to consider the priors in fixing penalty for present offense. *Spencer* v. *Texas* (1967).

BUT NOTE: Prior convictions that were secured in violation of *Gideon* v. *Wainwright* (assuring defendant right to counsel, even if indigent, absent intelligent voluntary waiver) cannot constitutionally be employed as a basis for increasing punishment under recidivism statute, for such convictions are deemed void under Due Process. *Burgett* v. *Texas* (1967).

m. *Fairness in obtaining photographic identification evidence:* Showing of photographs ("mug shots") of suspected criminals to witnesses in attempt to obtain identification evidence must be conducted in a way that is fair and calculated to obtain reliable evidence. The use of photographs to assist witnesses in identifying criminals is not *per se*, either unfair or unconstitutional. However, the technique and manner in which the photographs are used must be examined in each case to determine whether the procedures employed were "so impermissibly suggestive as to give rise to a very sustantial likelihood of irreparable misidentification." *Simmons* v. *United States* (1968).

n. *Police "lineup" procedures for identification pur-*

> *poses* must be conducted in a way that provides assurance against erroneous identification due to suggestive or unfair police tactics. Assurance that fair tactics were employed requires that counsel be given an opportunity to be present during lineup.

Example: Held that absence of counsel, during police lineup, absent intelligent waiver, denies constitutional right to effective counsel and precludes admission of identification testimony from the witnesses. The right to counsel being present at the lineup is essential to a fair trial at which the witnesses against the defendant can be meaningfully cross-examined, just as counsel's presence during custodial interrogation is necessary (see the *Miranda* case) to give meaningful protection to the accused's right not to incriminate himself. The lineup is a particularly critical point of the pretrial proceedings, because of the hazards of erroneous identification evidence, the possibilities of improper suggestive influences upon identification witnesses, and the difficulties at the trial of adequately depicting these factual events in an effort to challenge the credibility of identification testimony. The presence of defense counsel would often avert the possible unfairness of the line-up procedure and assure that a basis for effective cross-examination was provided the defendant at the trial. *United States* v. *Wade*, (1967); *Gilbert* v. *California* (1967).

NOTE: Other significant aspects of the "line-up" problem should be noted: Not only is testimony inadmissible to prove that a witness identified the defendant *at the lineup*, but it is also constitutionally improper to allow a witness to identify the defendant *within the courtroom* if the in-court identification is a product of the previous line-up at which counsel was not present. The former evidence is automatically to be excluded. The latter must be excluded as the fruit of the poisonous episode, unless the prosecution establishes by "clear and convincing evidence" that the in-court identification, on all the circumstances, had an independent source. *Gilbert* v. *California* (1967).

Even when the new rule does not apply—and presumably even when counsel is present at the lineup—the way in which the lineup is conducted may violate Due Process anyway, if it is shown to have been handled in a manner unnecessarily suggestive of the suspect's guilt, or in a way conductive to irreparable mistaken identification. This issue depends on the totality of all the circumstances of the case. *Stovall* v. *Denno* (1967).

Violations of the exclusionary rules relating to lineups where counsel was not present are subject to the "prejudicial error" doctrine. That is, admission of the identification testimony does not require automatic reversal of the conviction (as in coerced confession cases), but allows affirmance if the reviewing court is able to declare a belief that the error was harmless—did not contribute to the result—beyond a reasonable doubt. *Gilbert* v. *California* (1967).

GLOSSARY OF CRIMINAL LAW TERMS AND PHRASES

Abet To encourage or assist another to commit a crime; to assist in the preparation of a crime as aid and abet.

Abortion Procuring or causing a miscarriage.

Accessory Any person who *after* a felony has been committed, aids or conceals a principal to help him avoid arrest or prosecution.

Accomplice One who is liable for punishment as a principal because he advised, encouraged, aided, or participated in the commission of a crime.

Accusation A general term covering complaints, indictments, and informations.

Admission A statement by a person as to the existence of some fact.

Adultery Living in cohabitation with another as husband or wife if at least one of the partners is married to someone else.

Affidavit A declaration in writing sworn before a person who has authority to administer an oath.

Affirmation A formal declaration by a witness that he will speak truthfully. An affirmation has the same force and effect as an oath.

Appellate Court A higher court which hears appeals, not a trial court.

Arraignment The procedure by which a court informs an accused person of the charge against him, determines that he is the proper person wanted, tells him his legal rights, and asks for a plea (guilty or not guilty).

Arrest The taking of a person into custody in a case and in a manner authorized by law.

Asportation The removal of things from one place to another. The carrying away of goods such as is required in the offense of larceny.

Assault An unlawful attempt to inflict injury or apply force to another.

Attempt Intent plus overt act (beyond preparation) toward the commission of a crime.

Autopsy The dissection of a dead human body by an authorized person in order to determine the cause of death.

Bailiff An officer assigned to assist in keeping order in the court.

Battery Any willful and unlawful use of force or violence upon the person of another.

Bench Warrant A warrant issued by a judge for contempt of court, or for failure to appear in court.

Burglary Entering any kind of building for the purpose of committing theft or any felony. Forced entry is not required.

Carnal Knowledge Sexual intercourse; the act of a man having sexual contact with a female.

Certiorari A writ issued by a higher court directing an inferior court to send up to the form some pending proceeding, or all the records and proceedings for a review or trial of the pending issues.

Circumstantial Evidence Evidence from which the existence of another principal fact may be inferred or concluded.

Coercion Compulsion or force, as coercion to commit a crime.

Cohabitation Unmarried persons living together as husband and wife.

Commitment An official court order directing the taking of a person to a jail, prison, hospital, or other place for custodial residence.

Common Law The basis for American law, as derived from the laws of England.

Common Law Marriage Unmarried persons living together as husband and wife by mutual consent; not recognized in California (certain exceptions regarding validity in another state prior to arrival in this state). An extra-legal agreement to marry.

Complaint A charge of the commission of a crime, made to a court.

Compounding The crime of taking some reward for forbearing to assist in the prosecution of a criminal, or allowing him to escape.

Confession A complete acknowledgement of guilt of some crime.

Conspiracy A combination of two or more persons to commit a crime.

Contempt Willful disregard of the orders or process of a court or crime against the dignity of a court.

Contraband Goods that the law forbids to be sold or bought, imported or exported.

Coroner An officer whose duty is to determine the cause of all violent and unusual deaths.

Coroner's Jury A jury appointed by a coroner to determine the nature of a death.

Corpus Delicti The body of a crime. The elements that must be proven to convict a defendant of a crime.

Corroboration Additional evidence—usually to confirm or support the testimony of a witness.

Court Trial A trial in which the defendant waives his right to a jury in which case the judge decides the guilt or innocence.

Crime A public offense committed or omitted in violation of a law forbidding or commanding it, and to which is annexed any of the following five punishments: (1) death (2) imprisonment (3) fine (4) removal from office (5) disqualification to hold and enjoy any office of honor, trust, or profit.

Cross Examination The examination of a witness by the side that did not call him.

Cumulative Additional. In evidence terminology, cumulative evidence is that which is the same nature as other evidence and to the same fact.

Defendant One against whom a civil or criminal action has been brought.

Demurrer An answer to an accusation, not denying it, but stating that the accusation itself is defective or legally ineffective.

Direct Examination Examination of a witness by the side that calls him.

Double Jeopardy The fact of being officially accused and on trial for the same offense for the second time.

Duces Tecum From the Latin for "bring with you." Used to indicate a writ (subpoena duces tecum) which requires a party who is summoned to appear in court to bring with him some document, piece of evidence, or other thing to be used or inspected by the court.

Duress Coercion upon a person to do something against his will.

Dying Declaration A statement by a dying person as to cause of death and who was responsible; may be repeated by person hearing it in court, an exception to hearsay rule.

Emancipation The act by which one who was unfree, or under the power and custody of another (such as an unmarried child), is rendered free or set at liberty by his own master. In common practice, a child becomes emancipated from his parents by law when he reaches the age of maturity or marries.

Embezzlement The crime of taking money or other property entrusted to one, usually theft or misappropriation by an employee.

Entrapment Causing a criminal act for the purpose of instigating a criminal prosecution.

Evidence The means by which a fact is established or disproved. It usually consists of testimony of witnesses, documents and other things that can be seen, and the knowledge of the court.

Excusable Homicide Unintentional killing by accident or misfortune.

Execution The means of carrying out the orders of the Court usually against a person's body or goods, also applied to the formal killing of a person as a punishment for a crime.

Ex Post Facto A term applied to a law that seeks to punish acts that were committed before the law was passed, prohibited by the Constitution.

Extortion The taking of property from another by means of illegal threats, compulsion, or force—blackmail.

Extradition The legal process of bringing an accused or convicted person back from another jurisdiction, state, or country.

False Imprisonment Any unlawful restraint of a person's liberty or freedom of locomotion.

False Pretense A deceit used to unlawfully gain money or other property belonging to another.

Felony A major crime. A crime punishable by death or imprisonment in a state prison.

Fence A term used to describe a receiver of stolen property.

Forgery The false making or altering of a writing or document with intent to defraud.

Gaming A contract between persons by which they will gamble with dice, cards, or other contrivances.

Grand Jury A body of persons sworn to inquire into crimes and bring accusations against the suspected criminals.

Gross Negligence Great negligence.

Habeas Corpus A writ by which a court directs the body of a person to be brought before it, upon a claim or unlawful detention. Every person who is detained in a jail or elsewhere has a right to be brought before the court to have the court determine whether or not that detention shall continue.

Habitual Criminal A person sentenced to prison for a long term or for life becuase of two or more previous convictions.

Hearsay Evidence not personally known to the person giving it but heard by him from someone else.

Homicide The killing of a human being by another human being.

Immaterial Not important, not altering anything.

Impanel The process of selecting a jury.

Incest The intermarriage or sexual intercourse between persons more closely related than first cousins.

Indictment A formal accusation of a crime by a Grand Jury.

Information A formal accusation of crime presented by the District Attorney to the Superior Court, following the Preliminary Hearing.

Inquest An inquiry by a Court or Coroner into the cause of violent or unusual death.

Intent Motive is the reason of moving cause, intent is purpose of, resolve to do an act, e.g., in mercy killings, the motive is to relieve pain, the intent is to kill. Proof of intent is required; proof of motive is always helpful, but never required.

Irrelevant Not to the point, does not apply.

Judgment The official declaration by a court of their result of a lawsuit.

Judicial Notice The notice which a judge will take of facts of common knowledge without the necessity of proving them.

Jury Trial A trial in which the jury decides guilt or innocence, and the judge decides only the law applicable.

Justifiable Homicide Killing which was legal and necessary even though intentional.

Kidnapping The forcible stealing, taking, enticing, or carrying away of a human being for the purpose of extorting money or property.

Kleptomania An abnormal impulse to steal.

Larceny Another term for theft, permanently taking property.

Legal Insanity The inability to tell right from wrong, a defense to crime.

Libel A malicious publication, using signs or pictures, tending to blacken the memory of a dead person or the reputation of a living person—same as slander, except that slander is oral or spoken.

Lottery A scheme for the distribution of prizes by chance among the buyers of the chances; an illegal drawing.

Lynching In popular usage: the killing of an accused criminal by mob. Legally: The taking by means of a riot, any person from the lawful custody of any peace officer, is lynching.

Magistrate A Judge.

Mala in Se Wrongs in themselves; acts morally wrong; offensive against conscience.

Malum Prohibitum A prohibited wrong; a thing which is wrong because it is prohibited; an act which is not inherently immoral but becomes wrong because its commission is expressly forbidden by positive law.

Malice An evil intent; a wish to vex or annoy; the state of mind that makes an act criminal.

Malicious Mischief Maliciously injuring or destroying any real or personal property.

Manslaughter The unlawful killing of a person without malice; usually through negligence or in heat of passion.

Mayhem The crime of depriving another person of a part of or use of his body.

Mens Rea A guilty mind; a guilty or wrongful purpose; a criminal intent.

Misdemeanor A lesser crime, usually punishable by county-jail sentence or a monetary fine.

Modus Operandi The manner or method of operation of a criminal.

Motive Motive is the reason or moving cause. Intent is purpose or resolve to do an act, e.g., in mercy killings the motive is to relieve pain, the intent is to kill. Proof of intent is required, proof of motive is always helpful but never required.

Moulage A cast used to preserve evidence as of a tire track, footprint, etc.

Murder The unlawful killing of a human being with malice aforethought.

Nighttime The hours between sunset and sunrise.

Nolo Contendere Formal declaration by an accused person that he will not defend himself against the accusation.

Non Compos Mentis Not of sound mind, insane. This is a very general term, embracing all varieties of mental derangement.

Nuisance A condition that is annoying, or that interferes with the use of property by others, such as smell, a health hazard, traffic blockade, etc.

Ordinance A law or local application, usually that of a city or county.

Overt Act A physical act, as opposed to an act of the mind, from which intent to commit a crime can be implied.

Parole Release given to a convicted criminal upon certain conditions and after having served part of his sentence in an institution.

Peace Officer One who has complete police power.

Penal Code Criminal statutes.

Personal Property Money, goods, animals, clothing, vehicles, etc.

Perjury Knowingly giving false evidence or testimony while under oath.

Plaintiff One who is bringing a civil action; the one suing.

Plea The answer that the accused person makes to the charge against him such as, "guilty," or "not guilty," etc.

Police Power The broad power under which the state can restrain private rights for the general welfare.

Post Mortem After death; usually refers to an examination to determine cause of death.

Preliminary Examination An examination held before a magistrate to determine whether an accused person should be held on a criminal charge and whether or not a crime was actually committed.

Presumption In the law of evidence, an assumption that an act is so until the contrary is proved, such as the presumption of innocence.

Prima Facie Evidence which, unless contradicted, is sufficient to maintain a fact.

Principal All persons involved in any way with the initial commission of a crime, even if not present at the time.

Privileged Communication One that need not be given in evidence, as a communication between a spouse, a priest, or a lawyer.

Probation A system of letting a convicted man go free instead of imprisoning him on condition that he observe certain terms of that probation.

Prosecution The Court proceedings for convicting a criminal; sometimes also used for the group of persons so concerned, such as the staff of the District Attorney, as distinguished from the defense.

Psychotic A person having a serious mental disorder.

Quasi Almost; as if; similar to; for example, quasi-military.

Rape Sexual intercourse with female accompanied by force or deceit, or with a person under 18 years of age, mentally ill, or intoxicated.

Real Property Land and buildings.

Real Evidence Evidence furnished by physical things, rather than verbal description.

Recidivist An habitual criminal. One who has been convicted more than once of crime, misdemeanor, or delinquency; a confirmed criminal: a repeater.

Relevant In the law of evidence, having to do with, or relating to, the case in hand; pertinent (as relevant testimony).

Remand To send back into custody, to commit to jail.

Res Gestae Acts incidental to a main fact and explanatory of it. The words and acts done immediately before or after a crime are considered to be part of it in the law of evidence.

Restitution The giving back of a thing, or its value, to the lawful owner.

Robbery The felonious taking of personal property in the possession of another, from his person or immediate presence, and against his will, accomplished by means of force or fear.

Rout Whenever two or more persons, assembled and acting together, make any attempt or advance toward the commission of an act which would be a riot if actually committed, such assembly is a rout.

Seduction Unlawful sexual intercourse with a female induced by promise of marriage.

Slander Spoken words which are injurious to the reputation of another person.

Sodomy Sexual intercourse which is against nature, i.e., between men or with animals.

Specific Intent Proof that a crime was committed with a specific purpose in mind.

Stare Decisis "Adhere to the decisions." The concept of precedence is related to this term.

Statute A law passed by a legislative authority. This word is used to designate the written law as distinguished from the unwritten law.

Statutory Authorized or prohibited by statute or law.

Subornation Procuring another person to commit perjury.

Subpoena A court order commanding a witness to appear. A process by which the attendance of a witness in court is required.

Subpoena Duces Tecum A subpoena commanding a witness to appear and bring something such as required records or documents with him.

Substantive Law That part of the law which is enforced as opposed to the laws (rules) which are followed in enforcing the law, e.g., rules of evidence are procedural law.

Summons Court order informing someone that a complaint has been made against him and that he must appear at a stated time and place to answer the charge (used mostly in civil cases).

Suspended Sentence Sentence after conviction that allows the convicted person to remain at large provided he observes certain conditions.

Theft Any intentional taking of the personal property of another person against the will of such person with intent to permanently deprive the victim of his property or title thereto.

Tort An injury by one person to another for which the injured person may sue for damages as distinguished from a crime which the state punishes, a civil wrong.

Trespass Entry on another's ground without lawful

authority and doing some damage, however, inconsiderable, to his real property.

Trial The examination of a cause, civil or criminal, before a judge who has jurisdiction over it, according to the laws of the land.

Unlawful Assembly A disturbance by three or more persons meeting together with an unlawful purpose.

Usury The crime of charging excessive interest.

Uttering The offering of or presenting, or attempting to cash a false thing such as counterfeit money with knowledge of the falsity, and the passing of a false or fictitious check is called uttering.

Venue The place or political subdivision where a trial is held or should be held. The locality where the alleged events occurred that caused the suit.

Versus Against, usually abbreviated as (v.) *People* v. *Jones.*

Verdict The decision of a trial jury upon the facts presented to them.

Warrant An authority from a Court to a peace officer, usually directing the arrest of a criminal or suspected criminal.

Willfully Intentionally, deliberately (not necessarily an intent to do wrong or violate the law).

Subject Index

Case Index